\

William Shakespeare's

Making Sense of A Midsummer Nights Dream!

A Students Guide to Shakespeare's Play

Includes Study Guide, Biography, and Modern Retelling

BookCaps™ Study Guides

www.bookcaps.com

Cover Image © dedMazay - Fotolia.com

Table of Contents

STUDY GUIDE **4**

HISTORICAL CONTEXT 5

PLOT OVERVIEW 6

    Short Synopsis 6

    Detailed Synopsis 6

THEMES/MOTIFS 11

    Forbidden Love 11

    Perception 11

    Foolishness 11

    Reason and Love 11

    Night and Day 12

    Gender 12

    The Dream World 12

    The Supernatural 12

    Control and Manipulation 13

    Peace and Chaos 13

CHARACTER SUMMARIES 14

    Theseus (Fi-se-us) 14

    Hippolyta (Hip-pol-li-ta) 14

    Lysander (Li-san-der) 14

    Demetrius (De-me-trius) 14

    Helena (Hel-ena) 14

    Hermia (Her-mia) 15

    Titania 15

    Robin (Puck) 15

    Oberon 15

    Egeus (Eh-gee-us) 15

    The Mechanicals 16

SCENE SUMMARIES 18

    Act One 19

    Act Two 23

    Act Three 28

    Act Four 34

    Act Five 38

THE LIFE AND TIMES OF WILLIAM SHAKESPEARE **41**

THE TIMES SHAKESPEARE LIVED IN 42

SHAKEPEARE'S FAMILY 44

SHAKESPEARE'S CHILDHOOD AND EDUCATION 46

SHAKEPEARE'S ADULTHOOD 48

MODERN VERSION OF THE PLAY **52**

ACT 1 53

    Scene I 53

Scene II 77

ACT II 88

Scene I 88

Scene II 112

ACT III 128

Scene I 128

Scene II 149

ACT IV 195

Scene I 195

Scene II 217

ACT V 222

Scene I 222

Scene II 259

ABOUT BOOKCAPS **266**

Study Guide

Historical Context

William Shakespeare, playwright extraordinaire, lived in 16th to 17th Century England. He wrote an immense number of plays, including the still popular Hamlet, Macbeth, and Romeo & Juliet. Many of his plays were written as part of the Lord Chamberlain's Men—later known as the King's Men—who were a company of players, or actors. Although Shakespeare is synonymous with the Globe Theatre, a great number of his plays were performed at Blackfriars Theatre and at court for royalty and their guests. He was also a seasoned poet and is still celebrated for his 154 sonnets, including the popular Sonnet 18. The beginning lines are possibly the most quoted out of all the sonnets: "Shall I compare thee to a Summer's day? Thou art more lovely and more temperate." I bet you've heard those lines before!

The 16th and early 17th Centuries in England were periods of enormous wealth and strength. Shakespeare lived through the Spanish war, saw the end of Elizabeth the Virgin Queen's reign, and heralded in the reunification of the English and Scottish thrones under one monarch, King James VI. However, despite the Royal family's enormous wealth and rich noblemen in the upper classes, the poor were extremely poor. Famine, poor hygiene and the lack of wages created an environment full of disease, crime and pestilence. If you were poor during this time, you had mighty little to look forward to! Some would visit the theatre as a means to escape their lives if they could afford it, but they would only be able to afford standing room. Imagine standing up through an hour long play! Other entertainment available to the poor included watching executions, tormenting those placed in stocks and attending witch trials. A pretty grim past-time, but there was little else to do,

A Midsummer Night's Dream is still one of Shakespeare's most popular plays. Most historians believe that the play was written between the years 1590 and 1956, when it debuted on stage. It was performed secretly during the Puritan period that criticized and shut down plays rulers did not like at festivals and fairs. Once it was performed on main stages again, it did not gather many compliments due to its farcical and exaggerated style. Many thought it was a play best suited to being read on paper, rather than being performed on stage. This is due in part to the darned little character development and the sudden new direction for the play once the Mechanicals perform. Even Samuel Pepys, a famous member of Parliament at the time, called it a ridiculous play.

Usually, Shakespeare liked to touch on a specific source for his plays, but A Midsummer Night's Dream appears to be strangely without one. Despite this, the play references many texts, including his own Romeo & Juliet, and Chaucer's Canterbury Tales.

Despite criticisms that some have had, A Midsummer Night's Dream is still well loved and continues to be tweaked and adapted and performed. In the more modern world, the play has been adapted into ballet performances, musicals, films and has inspired many more fictional works. Its blend of the comic and fantasy are strong draws for many artists, especially those that have embellished and adapted the fairy world to enhance Shakespeare's work into a feast for the eyes!

Plot Overview

Short Synopsis

After given an ultimatum by her father, Egeus, and Theseus, the Duke of Athens, to marry Demetrius on their command or become a nun, Hermia and Lysander, her lover, run away into the woods. Helena, who is in love with Demetrius, decides to tell him where Hermia has gone to get his attention. At the same time, the warring monarchs of the fairy world—Titania and Oberon—quarrel over an Indian Boy. Their quarrel leads to mischief, trickery, misunderstandings. What follows in the Athenian woods is a chaotic love story that, unsurprisingly for a comedy, ends with three happy weddings and the reunification of the fairy world.

Detailed Synopsis

Theseus and Hippolyta discuss their impending wedding. They are interrupted by Egeus, a nobleman, who asks Theseus for his help with his daughter, Hermia. She refuses to marry Demetrius, who Egeus has picked out for her and wants to follow her heart and marry Lysander for love instead. Hermia is told she must marry Demetrius or become a nun. Demetrius and Lysander argue with one another; Lysander reveals that Demetrius has led another woman, Helena, on, and now she is in love with him.

Lysander begs Hermia to run away with him so they can elope. They decide to meet in the Woods at night, and Lysander leaves to avoid suspicion. Hermia tells Helena about their plan. After Hermia leaves, Helena reveals that she is in love with Demetrius and is jealous of Hermia's superior looks. She thinks this is the reason Demetrius loves Hermia more than he loves her. She decides to tell Demetrius about Hermia's elopement to get in his finest books. Maybe, she thinks, this will put her in a kinder light.

In the meantime, the Mechanicals—a group of workers in an amateur dramatics club—arrive at a space in Athens to rehearse their play together. Quince, the leader of the group, hands out parts. Bottom, who is to play the lead role of Pyramus in <u>Pyramus and Thisbe</u>, interrupts at every chance he gets to provide his opinion, or ask to play more roles than just the lead. Quince politely disagrees with him each time. The others—Flute, Snout, Snug, and Starveling—are handed their parts and bring up their insecurities with each. For example, Snug is worried he won't be able to remember his lines as the Lion, even though his lines are all roars! Once all the parts have been handed out, they decide to meet in the Woods away from everyone else so they can rehearse without being interrupted.

In the Woods, Robin Goodfellow and another fairy meet. They talk about the King and Queen of the fairy world arguing over a stolen Indian boy. Queen Titania refuses to hand him over to King Oberon. As a result, the natural world is in disorder: fog has spread across the land and crops refuse to grow. They reveal to each other that Titania and Oberon are both coming to the Woods. The Fairy wants Oberon to go away so he won't upset her Queen.

Titania and Oberon meet. Oberon asks her for the Indian boy. Titania refuses as the boy's mother was a dear friend of hers who died. She looks after him for her friend. Oberon wants her to be obedient, but Titania refuses him. Titania knows the only reason Oberon has returned to the Woods is to wish Theseus well in his marriage, and because Oberon is in love with Hippolyta. Titania tells her fairies to follow her, and they leave Oberon and Robin alone. Oberon asks Robin to fetch a flower hit with a stray bow from Cupid's arrow and bring it to him: he will use the flower juice to make Titania fall in love with the next thing she sees so he can take the boy from her.

As Robin fetches the flower, Demetrius enters the woods, followed by Helena. Neither sees Oberon as he hides from sight. Helena begs him to love her again, but Demetrius threatens to rape her. She doesn't care if he hurts her; she's already hurt by the fact that he won't pursue her. Demetrius threatens to leave her with the wild animals and escapes into the thick of the woods once more, Helena hot on his heels. Oberon promises Helena that she will be pursued by the end of the night.

Robin returns with the flower. Oberon tells him to smear it on the eyes of an Athenian youth in the Woods so that he will love her more than she loves him. Oberon leaves to smear the flower juice on Titania's eyes.

Titania asks her fairy court to sing her to sleep and stand guard while she sleeps. Once she has fallen asleep, all but one leaves to carry out errands. Oberon enters and smears the flower juice across her eyes. He tells her not to wake up until something disgusting comes near, and then to fall in love with it. Oberon leaves.

Lysander and Hermia stumble in. They are tired and lost in the Woods. They decide to lie down to rest for a while. Lysander wants to lie close to Hermia, but she tells him to be gentlemanly and sleep further away. Lysander disagrees—they are in love; their hearts are as one, and so they should sleep near one another. Hermia refuses once more, and Lysander gives in, although points out he only meant the suggestion innocently. They go to sleep.

Robin enters and smears the flower juice across Lysander's eyes and chastises Hermia for sleeping so closely to him.

Demetrius and Helena enter. Demetrius continues to threaten Helena's safety. She begs him to stay with her, even if it means killing her. Demetrius tells her that he'll leave her to the wild animals and runs away again. Helena is too tired to run after him and decides to lie down to sleep, but, before she can, she sees Lysander. He wakes up and immediately falls in love with her. Lysander wants to find Demetrius so he can kill him for Helena's heart. Helena thinks that Lysander is making fun of her. She runs away. Lysander tells the still sleeping Hermia not to wake up or follow him as she is too sweet for him now. He runs after Helena.

Hermia wakes after a terrifying nightmare in which her heart is being eaten by a snake, and finds herself alone. She calls out to Lysander, but he does not answer. Fearing the worst, she decides to try and find him.

The Mechanicals gather in the Woods for a rehearsal of the play. They discuss various elements in the play that they need—Moonshine and a Wall—and how best to represent these on stage. Bottom is also worried about using a sword on stage when Pyramus has to kill himself. He doesn't want to frighten the audience, and so they decide to write a Prologue to explain to the audience that the play isn't real. Snout is also worried about the Lion frightening the audience, and Bottom decides that he should speak to the audience instead of roar to reassure the ladies. Once these issues have been resolved, the actors start to rehearse. None of them are remarkably talented.

Robin enters and is at first upset that they are rehearsing so close to Titania, but is intrigued by the prospect of an entertaining play. He thinks that Bottom's Pyramus is the strangest portrayal he's ever seen, and follows him off "stage" behind some bushes. Bottom returns with a donkey's head instead of his own, transformed by Robin. The others flee frightened that the monster will attack them. Bottom thinks that they are trying to trick him into being upset and refuses to run away. He sings, which wakes Titania. She falls in love with him on sight. Bottom doesn't quite understand why she has fallen in love with him, but doesn't actually argue with her. Titania calls her most trusted fairies—Peaseblossom, Moth, Cobweb and Mustardseed—to take care of Bottom. They leave to go and sleep in a flowerbed.

Oberon wonders whether or not Titania has fallen in love with something horrid yet. Robin enters and reports that she has fallen in love with Bottom, who he has given a donkey's head, and the Athenian youth is also in love with Helena as requested. Oberon sees Demetrius and Hermia coming—Robin reveals he has never seen Demetrius before, and may have mixed up the Athenian men. Hermia thinks Demetrius has killed Lysander as there's no other reason why he would have left her, but Demetrius defends himself: he hasn't even seen Lysander. Hermia won't talk to him again and runs away into the woods. Demetrius doesn't want to go after her while she's upset and goes to sleep.

Oberon tells Robin off, sends him to fetch Helena, and smears flower juice across Demetrius' eyes so that he will fall in love with Helena. Demetrius wakes and declares his love for Helena when she enters. Helena believes that both of the Athenian men are in on the joke now, and is upset. Demetrius gives up on his claim for Hermia and tells Lysander to go marry her instead, but Lysander doesn't want her either.

Hermia enters and asks Lysander where he went. He followed his love: Helena. Helena accuses Hermia of persuading the boys to trick her, but Hermia doesn't understand. They quarrel with one another, and once Hermia realizes Lysander genuinely does mean what he says; she threatens to beat Helena up. Demetrius and Lysander, too, decide to duel for Helena's hand.

Helena tries to reason with Hermia--she loves Hermia. They grew up together! Hermia tells her to leave. Helena does, afraid that Hermia will attack her. Demetrius and Lysander leave to fight one another further away in the woods. Hermia doesn't know what to think anymore. She leaves.

Oberon blames Robin for the mess he's made. Robin assures him that he made a mistakes. Oberon asks Robin to make the Woods dark so the two Athenian men won't be able to see one another to fight, and imitate their voices to lure them away from one another. He gives Robin a new flower to smear across their eyes and undo the damage he has caused. When the youths wake up, they will think of the night as if it were all a dream. Oberon plans to do the same for Titania after she gives him the Indian boy. They have to work fast to complete the work before the impending sunrise!

Lysander and Demetrius, still trying to find one another, follow Robin around the Woods. He uses their voices to call to them alternately until they both grow tired. They both lie down to sleep. Helena and Hermia, in separate areas of the Woods, decide to sleep as well, exhausted and weary from the trying night. Robin smears the flower juice on Lysander's eyes to cure him and bids them all to find the one they truly love when they wake.

While the others sleep, Titania and Bottom enter with her fairies. She dotes on him, scratching his ears and threading flowers in his hair. Bottom wishes nothing more than to sleep, and so Titania tells her fairies to leave them alone, and curls up with Bottom in a flowerbed.

Oberon and Robin, hidden from view, talk about Oberon's meeting with Titania. He managed to persuade Titania to hand over the Indian boy with no problem. After he releases Titania from the spell—for Oberon wants her to see what a fool he has made of her—Oberon wants Robin to remove Bottom's donkey head. Titania wakes up and is horrified to find that she was in love with Bottom, and never wants to see him again. Robin gives Bottom his human head back. While the Athenians sleep, Oberon and Titania dance together. Oberon is overjoyed; he has Titania back and is convinced that there will be three weddings the next day. Robin interrupts them: the night is almost over! Oberon and Titania leave for the other side of the world to catch up with the night.

Theseus and Hippolyta enter with servants and Egeus. They talk about a epic hunt they have planned, and praise the ability of hunting dogs to bark loudly enough for it to echo off cliffs and trees. Theseus suddenly sees the Athenians sleeping on the ground. He wakes them up with the servants' horns. Theseus assumes they are out in the Woods because they knew Theseus would be there, but questions Lysander and Demetrius as to why two enemies could sleep so closely to one another. They have no idea how they got there, but do remember running into the woods. Although Egeus calls for Lysander to be arrested upon hearing he planned to elope with Hermia, Demetrius interrupts with his version of the events and proclaims his love for Helena. He doesn't know how exactly it has happened, but his love for Hermia seems to have disappeared. Theseus refuses to uphold Egeus' wish and will allow the two happy couples to marry one another. They give up on hunting now that the day is running into the afternoon, and head back to Athens for the weddings. All but the four Athenians leave; they're not sure if they're awake yet or not, but decide they must be if they all saw Theseus. They decide to compare dreams along the way to Athens.

After they leave, Bottom awakes. He can't put into words what he just experienced, but will get Quince to write it down for him.

Back in Athens, the Mechanicals lament the loss of Bottom. They don't know where he is, and assume he has been kidnapped. They're upset that the play won't be put on as Bottom was the only person fit to play Pyramus. While they compliment his characteristics, Snug arrives to tell the group that there have been three couples married that day. Bottom arrives! He won't tell them what happened to him just yet as they need to get ready for the play!

Theseus, Hippolyta and Philostrate discuss the strange things the Athenian youths have been saying. Theseus believes it sounds downright made up and blames love for their hallucinations. Hippolyta wonders if it wasn't a dream as their dreams were all the same.

Demetrius, Helena, Lysander and Hermia arrive. After an exchange of blessings, Theseus calls on Philostrate to list the entertainment he has planned for the wedding party. Theseus rejects a few—including a retelling of Hercules and the Centaurs—but asks to see Pyramus and Thisbe. Philostrate warns them against it as he watched them rehearse earlier; they were awful! Theseus still wants to see it, and so Philostrate leaves to fetch them. Hippolyta doesn't want to laugh at poor people, but Theseus assures her that they will be respectful and compliment what they do well.

The play begins. It's a bit of a shamble: the actors explain exactly what is happening on stage rather than acting out the story. After a brief Prologue telling the audience they are not there to entertain them, Pyramus and Thisbe talk through the Wall, played by Snout, who holds up his two fingers to form a chink in the wall. The two lovers plan to meet at Ninny's tomb. In a series of asides to one another, Hippolyta, Theseus and Demetrius criticize or compliment the actors. Hippolyta thinks this play is the silliest she's ever seen.

Snug as the Lion appears on stage and explains to them that he's not actually a Lion. The Moon enters, carrying a lantern and explains rather confusingly that he is the man in the moon and the lantern is the moon. Demetrius jokes that he would like to see how the man could fit into the lantern so easily, but the Moon continues on regardless. Meanwhile, Thisbe is frightened by the Lion, who tears her cloak off and rips it.

Pyramus finds Thisbe's cloak and assumes she has been killed and stabs himself with his sword. Hippolyta hopes Thisbe won't cry over Pyramus too much as he isn't truly worth it. Thisbe finds Pyramus and stabs herself. Breaking character, Bottom asks if the audience wants to hear the Epilogue, but Theseus thinks that a play where all the main characters have died doesn't need an Epilogue; there's no-one left to blame!

Theseus congratulates them on their performance, and then announces to the others that it is time for bed.

Robin steps in. He talks about the ghoulish and supernatural things that happen when night comes. He has been sent ahead to clean the house and make sure no one disturbs the sleeping Athenians before the fairies arrive. Oberon and Titania sing and dance together to bless the house, the marriages, and the couples' future children. They all leave but Robin, who addresses the audience. He asks them to think of the play as a kind of dream if it has offended them. If they give him a chance, he can set things right, and if he doesn't set things right he will be called a liar. He asks the audience to applaud if they are still friends, and then leaves.

Themes/Motifs

Forbidden Love

In Act One Scene One, Lysander discusses the ways that love has been forbidden throughout history, either through age difference or class separation. Hermia's love is forbidden by her father, Egeus. Helena's love is forbidden by her beloved Demetrius. Titania forbids Oberon to come near her again because of their quarrel and refuses to hand over the Indian boy. In The Mechanical's play, Thisbe and Pyramus are forbidden to see one another, and even lose their lives before they can be together.

Perception

The flower juice that is smeared on Lysander and Titania's eyes changes their view of the world. It even changes their heart. They no longer see what they saw before. The humans—aside from Bottom—never see the fairy world, even though Robin and Oberon are often watching over them. The moon, which provides light for many of them, does not help illuminate the woods while Robin teases and taunts Lysander and Demetrius through the shadows. They think they're following one another, but they're actually being tricked by Robin.

Foolishness

Bottom, even in his name, is quite a foolish character. Although many of the workmen putting on the play have moments of stupidity, Bottom's arrogance coupled with his utter ignorance paint him as a man who thinks he's the best at everything he attempts, when actually he's quite awful. That the others are duped into believing Bottom is a fantastic performer only adds to the comedy. When Bottom is given a donkey's head, he physically represents folly.

Later on the performers of the play do not even realize that they're performing incorrectly—i.e by explaining to the audience what is happening rather than showing them—and do not realize they are being mocked by Theseus and the rest of the audience. But it's not just Bottom who is an intensely foolish character; Hermia and Helena have an argument about their contrasting heights without Helena realising that she's picking on Hermia for it, and Demetrius can be called a fool for believing he loves Hermia enough to reject Helena, who he arguably knew he loved.

Reason and Love

When Bottom comments that reason and love do not go well together (3.1), he simplifies a common thread of investigation in the play. It seems that none of the players in Midsummer follow reason closely when faced with their love, or when following their heart's desire, and those that are questioned over their choice of love are often faced with statements others believe to be logical. For example, Egeus' attempts to control his daughter's heart are down to his role as a Father. Only when Theseus sees that there is no more claim on Hermia from Demetrius does he overrule societal law and let love win.

The mess that is made with the flower liquid suggests that love is illogical, ever changing, and can transform humans into blind, cruel people if they don't keep their heads. Even though it is reason that turns Hermia away into the woods, setting the events in action, and love that resolves their conflict, Theseus still rejects the lovers' remembrance of their dream as silly imagination. He rejects their memory in favour of reason. It is also reason that brings everything back under control, which suggests that maybe reason and love need to go together for a couple to survive.

Night and Day

Seeing by the light of the moon, or meeting under starlight might be considered romantic, but the night sky is actually indicative of the presence of the fairy world. Oberon admits that he does like the Sun, but he prefers to fly around at night. He also admits that their mischief must be undone and made right before daylight, suggesting some predetermined rules for their kind. When Titania meets with him, and the dawn comes, they leave for the darker side of the world. In many ways, the darkness of the night allows the fairies to cause mischief and fun. The day, and light, on the other hand, is the world of the humans. They wake at first light, and are in charge of what happens to them during this time, while the four Athenian youths and Bottom had no choice what was done to them throughout the night by the fairies.

Gender

Hermia and Helena threaten to attack one another over men despite the fact that they grew up together, and have obviously been close friends. They both fawn over the men that they love and chase them through the woods. Titania is tricked by her husband, Oberon, and made a fool of because she won't do as she is told when asked to give up the Indian boy. Despite the fact that Bottom has a donkey's head for much of the play, he seems less of a fool than Titania who calls him beautiful and embraces him in the flowerbeds. And Demetrius, though he chases Hermia into the woods to take her back from Lysander, threatens Helena with rape and murder if she doesn't stop following him. Even though she doesn't listen to him, his threats represent the distinct control men believe they have over women in this play.

The Dream World

A dreaming Hermia believes she sees Lysander sitting by as her heart is eaten, which is a strong metaphor for what has happened while she has been asleep. When she wakes up though, she has no idea where Lysander has gone. Just as the world is under a kind of fog, so too is reality. Titania wakes to find that she has had an awful dream about being in love with a donkey, and the Athenians remember the night in the woods as a dream under Oberon's command. It is in the world of dreams and the mystic that brings the most clarity.

The Supernatural

Although the Supernatural elements in the play can be blamed for the chaotic events and misunderstanding between the Athenians in the woods, magic ultimately resolves the problems between them and bring about a happy end for both couples. And, even though Oberon has to use magic to trick Titania into giving him the Indian boy, this resolves the argument between them and brings the natural world back to order once more.

Control and Manipulation

Egeus wants to control who his daughter, Hermia, marries. This way, he would be able to control not only her heart, but her body. Helena wants to control Demetrius and make him love her, just as Demetrius wants Hermia to love him, but Helena also suspects that it is Hermia who has manipulated the two men into pretending to love her. Although not revealed explicitly, its suggested that Hippolyta has been coerced into marrying Theseus because she lost the war to him; she isn't marrying him for love.

Peace and Chaos

Due to the war between Oberon and Titania, the seasons and weather are at odds with one another. Titania laments the loss of farmer's crops, and the fog that has crept over the world because of their fights. It seems that until the two fairy monarchs resolve their issues, the world will continue to be chaotic in nature. That chaos bleeds over into the other people in the play, especially the Athenian youths lost in the woods. In the human world, the threat Hermia represents is the undoing of the peace in her family by refusing to marry Demetrius at her father's command.

Character Summaries

Theseus (Fi-se-us)

Theseus is the Duke of Athens. Theseus himself may be based on the famous Greek God, who was the mythical King who founded Athens, and the total hero of the Athenian people. He is generally fair and just, because he overrides Egeus' wishes to force his daughter to marry Demetrius once the four lovers have sorted their problems out. He is also a man of law and society; he follows the rules of warfare in that he marries Hippolyta, and grants Egeus his initial request to force Hermia to decide between Demetrius and becoming a nun. However, he is also another example of the power that man has over woman in <u>Midsummer</u>, for he has not won Hippolyta's heart and hand in marriage honourably, but in the battlefield.

Hippolyta (Hip-pol-li-ta)

Hippolyta, the Queen of the Amazons, is due to marry Theseus after she and her army were defeated in battle. We don't see or hear much from her, probably due to her subserviency to Theseus after she has lost the war, but what we do find out is that she is mildly protective of the common man. This could be because she feels uncomfortable around them. She comments that she doesn't want to watch the play if they're going to mock the actors for their own entertainment. This could be Shakespeare's way of using the female presence as a place of sympathy, but it could also be due to her empathy as someone who has been trapped.

Lysander (Li-san-der)

Lysander is in love with Hermia and will not stand down despite the threats to his safety made by Demetrius and Hermia's father, Egeus. It can be assumed that Lysander is quite romantic, as he not only discusses numerous forbidden loves, but also wants to steal Hermia away into the night to elope with her. Lysander seems used to using his soft and gentle manner to persuade people into giving him what he wants, as he tries this with Hermia when they lie down together in the wood. When he is threatened by Demetrius, however, his masculine nature appears once more, suggesting that masculinity is the stronger of the sexes.

Demetrius (De-me-trius)

Demetrius is a bit of a scoundrel: he fell in love with Helena, and then changed his mind and decided he wanted Hermia instead. He threatens Helena in the woods after she chases him with not only rape, but also death. He leaves her alone in the woods to fend for herself because he wants to find Hermia, and yet through all this Helena sticks by him. He also joins in with the criticisms of the play with Theseus, so it can be assumed— although we don't see much evidence of it—that he is always looking for the Duke's approval. Either that, or Demetrius just majorly enjoys being nasty.

Helena (*Hel-ena*)

An Athenian lady. It would be an understatement to say that Helena suffers from low self esteem; she constantly puts herself down because of her physical attributes, and for her personality. She claims she cries too much and blames this on her poor features. She grew up with Hermia and has probably been in quiet competition with her since they met, as her fears and insecurities appear unusually deep seated. Helena is extremely love-sick for Demetrius, who she was engaged to before he fell in love with Hermia. Even though her loyalty to Demetrius can be seen as a sign of weakness, especially when he threatens to rape her, she shows her cleverness in the plan to get him back through giving him information, and in her refusal to believe Lysander loves her.

Hermia (Her-mia)

The second of the Athenian ladies, Hermia is well loved by all. She is called beautiful, so we can assume that she has had many suitors, from which Demetrius has been chosen for her. She's forthright in her belief that she should be able to marry for love, and is brave enough to take what would be a terrifying step away from her father and everything she knows for love.

Titania

The Queen of the Fairies, Titania starts off as a strong ruler who will not bow to her husband's wishes due to her morality. She will not give up the Indian Boy just because he wants him, and has made a vow to her friend and the boy's mother. And yet, after Titania is made a fool of, and she is tricked into handing back the Indian Boy, she takes Oberon back without much any argument. From then on, she takes his orders, dances with him and is generally amenable. Although it could be argued that this is evidence of male dominance, it could also represent Titania's nurturing side. She refuses to follow Oberon's orders because her maternal instincts tell her not to, and once she no longer has to worry for the boy; she can forgive Oberon easily.

Robin (Puck)

Robin, or Puck as he is often known, is a complete mischief maker and the trickster personified. He is a servant to Oberon and is sent to fetch flowers, run errands and smear the flower juice across the Athenian youth's eyes. Robin, in essence, gets many of the events of the play rolling and is quite a prominent character for this reason. Some historians have even pinpointed Robin as the protagonist of Midsummer as the play is without a clear lead. Although he plays cruel tricks on Bottom by giving him a donkey's head, he is generally a kindhearted character and will admit to mistakes he has made. Robin is a fairy, but he is not as gentle and sweet as Titania's servants; instead, he is a little more rough around the edges.

Oberon

The King of the Fairies. He, like Theseus and Egeus, believe that they can and should be able to control their wives, and is gobsmacked that his wife, Titania, continues to refuse him. He does not take delight in mischief that is not specifically designed by him or goes against true love; for example, Robin pours the flower juice on the wrong person's eyes. If the mischief is advantageous to him-for example when getting the Indian Boy back-he delights in it as long as they follow the rules of their world.,

Egeus (Eh-gee-us)

Hermia's father, and an Athenian courtier. He wants to control his daughter as per societal law to force her to marry the person he has chosen for her. He looks to Theseus a lot for help in these matters, but concedes to his rule once he is told Hermia will marry the person she loves.

The Mechanicals

Nick Bottom

Bottom is a well respected man among his peers, even if those peers are not to be well respected by the audience of <u>Midsummer.</u> They believe he is the smartest and best looking among them, which of course means he will end up with the lead in the play. Bottom interrupts Quince constantly to preen and prattle on about his abilities as a speaker or dramatist, which doesn't lend him much respect from the reader. We're meant to laugh at him. When Robin watches him rehearse Pyramus' role, he is called a strange and stupid actor; Robin's immediate thought is to give him a donkey's head, an animal which is often used to represent foolishness. Despite his ignorance, Bottom does mean well, and the rest of the group do look to him for help, which he is always there to provide.

Peter Quince

Quince is the real leader of the drama group, and a carpenter by trade. He knows how to deal with Bottom's constant interruptions and attempts to take over direction either by changing the subject, asking Bottom directly for his advice or by refusing his suggestion wholly through compliments. For instance, Quince tells Bottom he is the only one who could play Pyramus, and so he couldn't possibly play other characters. A terrifically skilled manipulator! Beyond this, not much else is known about his character.

Francis Flute

Flute is a bellows-mender and plays Thisbe in the play at the end. He is reluctant to play a female character and claims this is because he has a beard coming (1.2.40-41) and doesn't want to shave it off. Quince waves him off and tells him that he'll wear a mask over his face, and that's that. Flute doesn't argue much, and when he does speak it is usually to worry or compliment someone. He appears to be quite a nervous person.

Snug

Snug, the joiner, plays the Lion and is excited by the prospect. He is, however, afraid of frightening the ladies in the audience, which shows his gentleness and sensitivity. Snug can be seen as another foolish character, as he is initially worried he won't be able to learn his lines—which are at the time all roars! He is the only minor character of the Mechanicals not given a first name.

Tom Snout

Snout, the tinker, plays the Wall in the play. Initially he is meant to play Pyramus' father, but the play's need for a Wall ended up being greater. He, like his friends and fellow actors, is terrified by the prospect of Bottom being transformed, but is one of only two to return and approach Bottom for a short while. Snout's bravery is short lived, however, as once he has pointed out Bottom's transformation, he flees to safety.

Scene Summaries

Act One

Act One, Scene One

In Athens, surrounded by an attending court including Philostrate, an official, Theseus, the Duke of Athens and Hippolyta, Queen of the Amazons, discuss their upcoming wedding. They will measure the days left by the waxing of the moon: they have four days before their marriage takes place. Theseus has captured Hippolyta after he defeated the Amazons in a fierce battle; now that he has defeated her with his sword, he intends to defeat her in other ways. With love!

Theseus asks Philostrate to make the Athenian youths happy, and draw them out of their sadness. He leaves to do so. As Theseus continues to express his promises to Hippolyta, they are interrupted by visitors. It is Egeus, an Athenian courtier, with his daughter, Hermia, and her two suitors. He begs for Theseus to force his daughter to marry Demetrius, who he has given permission to marry his daughter. The only problem is that Hermia is in love with Lysander, who Egeus claims has put a spell over his daughter to make her disobey him. He accuses Lysander of pretending to be in love with Hermia, and then asks Theseus for his right as a father: to either force Hermia to marry Demetrius or to kill her for her disobedience.

Theseus asks for Hermia's opinions but warns her to think carefully because Egeus is her father, and should be a God to her. Hermia claims Lysander is as worthy as her father is and wishes that he could see things from her point of view, but Theseus chastises her for this—she must see things from her father's perspective. Theseus tells her to think carefully about her decisions: either she will be locked away as a pure and holy nun, or die a happily married woman. Hermia would rather be locked away than lose her virginity to a man she doesn't love. Theseus gives her time to think: by the time he and Hippolyta marry she has to decide between becoming a nun, death, and marrying Demetrius.

Lysander and Demetrius argue between themselves. Lysander tells him to go marry Egeus as he loves Demetrius so much. Lysander begs Egeus to see his side: he loves Hermia, which should count for more than what Demetrius can provide. He reveals Demetrius has been seeing Helena and now Helena loves him! Theseus admits he had heard about this, but had not had time to ask Demetrius yet. Theseus asks Demetrius and Egeus to come with him to talk about something and gives Hermia a final warning to think about her decision. Everyone leaves but Lysander and Hermia.

Lysander comments on Hermia's pale face. She is upset. Lysander tells her not to worry—that throughout history love has overcome many obstacles. Lysander reminds her that sometimes love has to overcome differences in class, or age, or relies on the opinions of others. Hermia thinks these are all awful things to have to face, but stand as enough reason for them to fight for their love too. Hermia and Lysander plan to meet each other in the woods the following night so they can run away to his Aunt's house and marry.

Helena comes in. They politely disagree with one another as to which of them is the most beautiful. Helena is upset that Demetrius prefers Hermia and is jealous of her beauty, voice, and eyes. She would give the entire world to have Demetrius for herself. She asks Hermia's advice for how to get Demetrius' attention, but Hermia doesn't actually know what she's done; she frowns at him and he still loves her! Helena wishes she could smile as well as Hermia frowns! Helena blames Hermia's beauty for Demetrius refusing to pay her any attention. Hermia tells her not to worry; she won't be around for too much longer as she and Lysander are running away! She and Lysander tell Helena exactly where they will be meeting. Hermia asks her to pray for them and hopes she and Demetrius finally fall in love, and then disappears, claiming she and Lysander can't be seen together just in case they are found out. Lysander then leaves.

By herself, Helena laments her situation. She knows other people in Athens think she is just as pretty as Hermia, but it doesn't matter because Demetrius doesn't think so. They are both obsessed with someone they can't have. She is upset that Demetrius promised to love her forever before he met Hermia, and so to get back at her, she'll tell Demetrius about their plan to run away and elope. Hopefully Demetrius will be grateful to her for the information, which will be worth it in her fight against her rival, Hermia.

Act One, Scene Two

The artists who will perform at Theseus and Hippolyta's wedding party rehearse. Quince, Snug, Bottom, Flute, Snout and Starveling gather together and listen as Quince hands out positions in the play. Bottom generally interrupts at every possible moment. He asks Quince to tell them the name of the play, which is A Very Tragic Comedy About the Horrible Deaths of Pyramus and Thisbe. Bottom will play the title role of Pyramus, who kills himself for love.

Bottom claims he will make the audience cry endlessly, bids Quince to name the other actors, and then interrupts to deliver his lines. Bottom believes his performance was truly inspirational. Quince doesn't respond and continues to carry on giving out the parts to the actors. Flute is to play Thisbe, Pyramus' lover, but he doesn't want to because he has a beard growing. Quince tells him that he can wear a mask, which prompts Bottom to ask to play Thisbe, as well as Pyramus, wearing a mask when required. Quince refuses: he'll play Pyramus, no one else. Quince gives out the rest of the roles: Robin as Thisbe's mother, Snout as Pyramus' father, Quince as Thisbe's father and Snug in the part of the Lion.

Snug is worried he won't be able to learn his lines, but Quince assures him all he needs to do is roar. Bottom wants to play the Lion as well because he'll roar so well that the Duke will ask him to roar again. Quince believes his roar might scare the Duchess and her ladies; they would be put to death! Bottom will roar gently then. Quince once again tells him that he will play the part of Pyramus and no other because he's the only one who could play such a handsome man. Bottom finally agrees to just play Pyramus and asks Quince what kind of beard he should have, but Quince doesn't genuinely care. Bottom lists the different kinds of beards he could have, but Quince points out that not all French people have beards, and he could play it clean shaven.

Quince hands out the scripts and asks them to learn their lines by the next night, and meet him in the woods a mile out of town in the moonlight. This is to avoid people interrupting or watching them while they rehearse. He asks them not to fail him. Bottom promises that they will be there and work hard. Quince tells them to meet by the giant oak tree in the Duke's woods. They leave.

Act Two

Act Two, Scene One

In the wood near Athens, a Fairy and Robin Goodfellow meet. Robin asks her where she is going; she tells him that she has gone everywhere. She works for Titania, the Fairy Queen. She bids him farewell as the Queen and her followers will arrive soon. Robin warns her that King Oberon is planning to throw a party in the area that night, and that she should keep the Queen away. He's upset with her because she's stolen a boy from an Indian King, and Oberon wants the boy to accompany him while they travel through the wild forests. The Queen, he reveals, has refused to give him the boy, and now they won't talk to each other.

The Fairy asks if he's Robin Goodfellow, who she has heard of. She accuses him of being mischievous, scaring the ladies in the nearby village, keeping people lost at night and stealing the cream from the top of milk. She reveals he is also sometimes called Puck, or Hobgoblin, and those who call him these names receive virtuous deeds from him. Robin admits it: he tells jokes to Oberon, pretends to be a stool and makes people fall over, and generally takes part in mischief. He announces Oberon is approaching. The Fairy wishes he would go away because Titania is also arriving.

On either sides of the wooded area, Titania and Oberon enter with their courts. They are not pleased to see each other. Titania asks her Fairies to make Oberon leave, but he makes them wait a moment; surely she should be obedient to her husband? She points out that if she has to be faithful to him, then he should be faithful to her, and not spend his days in the fields with other girls. Titania goes on to point out that the only reason he has returned is to wish Theseus well in his marriage to Hippolyta, who was once his own love. Oberon is shocked that she hasn't bothered to mention her own love for Theseus. She has even interfered in Theseus' past love life to break up his relationships!

Titania points out that their constant bickering has had an enormous impact on the world around them: fogs have risen up, and corn has rotted, diseases are rife, no one sings anymore, and the seasons have changed their characteristics. Oberon promises that all these wrongs will be put right as long as she hands over the Indian boy to him. The boy's mother was a follower and friend of Titania's and died during childbirth, and so she takes care of him instead for her sake. Oberon asks Titania how long she intends on staying in the woods. She will only stay until after Theseus is married. After Oberon once again asks for the boy, Titania calls her fairies to follow her away from this place otherwise she will continue to argue with him.

Oberon asks Robin to fetch him a flower hit by a stray arrow from Cupid's bow that was aimed at a woman under a vow of chastity. Liquid from the flower when smeared on the eyelids of a sleeping person will make a man or woman fall in love with the next person they see. Oberon wants this done fast; Robin will move fast enough to circle the earth in 40 minutes!

Robin leaves Oberon alone. In an aside, Oberon reveals that plans to use this on Titania to make her fall in love with the next thing she sees so that he can take the Indian boy from her. He doesn't even care if she falls in love with a bull, wolf or lion! Hearing Demetrius and Helena approaching, Oberon makes himself invisible.

Demetrius tells Helena to go home and stop pursuing him—he doesn't love her. He is looking for Lysander and Hermia, but is finding it difficult to find them. Helena will love him no matter what he does, despite how unworthy she thinks she is. Demetrius warns her that she is in a difficult and dangerous situation with a man she should not trust: he could rape her and take her virginity. Helena does not think of herself as alone because he is the entire world to her. Demetrius threatens to run away from her and leave her to wild animals. She'll still run after him. Demetrius begs her to leave him alone, and once again threatens to hurt her. Helena tells him that he's already hurt her—women, she believes, aren't meant to pursue men, but to be pursued! Demetrius leaves, followed by Helena who doesn't mind if she dies by the hand of the person she loves.

Oberon promises Helena she'll be the one who is pursued by the end of the night. Robin returns with the flower. He describes a place covered with growing flowers where Titania sleeps. Oberon will go there and smear a little part of the flower onto her eyelids. He gives a part of the flower to Robin and asks him to spread it across an Athenian man's eyes so that the next thing he'll see is Helena. He wants it done so that he'll love her more than she loves him. They leave, going in separate directions.

Act Two, Scene Two

Titania enters with her Fairies. She asks them to sing her to sleep before they go off to complete their work. They do, warning away snakes and other nasty things while their Queen sleeps. One of them stands guard over her while the others fly away to do their work.

Oberon enters and smears the flower juice across Titania's eyelids. He tells her to fall in love with the first thing that she sees when she wakes up, and bids her to wake up only when something nasty wanders by her. Oberon leaves.

Lysander and Hermia enter. He admits that he doesn't know where they are and is worried about how pale Hermia is. He suggests that they rest for a while to regain their strength, which Hermia agrees to. She'll sleep against a tiny hill, and tells Lysander to find something to sleep against, as well. Lysander disagrees; they'll sleep against the hill together because their love makes them one. Hermia isn't so sure she wants Lysander so close and asks him to sleep further away. Lysander assures her that he only meant it innocently. He believes that two hearts that love each other can be seen as one heart. They are connected by their vow of faith and should sleep close by. Hermia once again refuses: she wants to behave as they should. She is, however, thankful for his love, and wishes that it will always be this strong for her. Lysander agrees, and the two go to sleep.

Robin enters, still trying to find the Athenian youth to smear the flower juice on. He sees Lysander and Hermia and realizes that they must be the people he's been looking for. He smears the juice across Lysander's eyes and chastises Hermia for sleeping so close to someone so cruel. Robin adds another charm to the juice to prevent Lysander from being able to sleep again because of his overwhelming love. Robin leaves to find Oberon.

Demetrius enters, chased by Helena, who begs him to stay still even if it's to kill her. Demetrius tells her to leave, but Helena is afraid of being left alone. He couldn't possibly leave her alone in the woods! Demetrius leaves, telling her to find her own way as he's going to continue trying to find Hermia.

Helena is exhausted from chasing Demetrius. She wonders aloud how Hermia's eyes are so much brighter than hers—she assumes its because Hermia does not need to cry as much, whereas she is always upset. She compares herself to a bear, as even beasts run away from her in fear when they meet; of course Demetrius would run away from her when she looks like a monster. Suddenly she sees Lysander lying on the ground. After a brief moment of fear that he is actually dead, she bids Lysander wake up.

He does—when he sees Helena he proclaims his love for her! Lysander wonders where Demetrius is for he wants to run a sword through him and kill him. Helena tells him that he doesn't need to kill Demetrius because Hermia loves him, and for that he should be happy. Lysander doesn't understand why he would be happy with Hermia. To him, she's boring. It's more than logical to love Helena more than Hermia. His reason now guides him instead of his desire, and now he can see all love stories in her eyes.

Instead of believing him, Helena thinks he's making fun of her. She is upset that not only will she never be able to have Demetrius, but that Lysander has to treat her like this. She thought Lysander was much kinder than this. Before she leaves, she once again tells him that it is terribly cruel for a man to emotionally abuse her after another has already rejected her. She flees.

Lysander realizes that Helena had not seen Hermia. He begs Hermia not to wake up or come near him again—she is too sickly sweet for him to stomach anymore. Citing the fact that it was a complete mistake to ever fall in love with Hermia, he'll work hard to find Helena and serve her. He leaves.

Hermia wakes up, thick in the middle of a nightmare about a snake eating her heart while her beloved Lysander watched on. She calls out for Lysander, who is not there. She calls again, but he does not answer. Hermia decides to find him, or die in the process.

Act Three

Act Three, Scene One

As Titania sleeps on, Quince and the other players gather. Bottom checks that they are all present. They are. Quince proclaims that this area is perfect for their rehearsals, and they will practice the play in full before they perform in front of the Duke. Bottom, as always, interrupts. He's worried that some things in the play won't work. For instance, Pyramus has to kill himself with a sword, but he's concerned this will upset the ladies in the audience. Some of them agree, and fear they will have to leave out all the killing, but Bottom has an idea. He wants to recite a prologue to assure the audience that no one is going to be hurt during the play and that they're not actually Pyramus and Thisbe, and so on, but actors playing the parts. Quince agrees, but he and Bottom disagree regarding the number of syllables in the lines that will be written.

Snout is still worried the Lion will scare the ladies. Bottom agrees: there's nothing scarier than a Lion! Snout suggests adding another Prologue, but Bottom won't have that. Snout will simply show his face in the costume's neck, and talk directly to the audience to let them know he isn't a real Lion.

Quince is worried about the moonlight they will need to bring into a room as Thisbe and Pyramus meet by moonlight. Snout asks if the moon will be shining that night. They gather a calendar to double check: thankfully, it is. Bottom suggests leaving a window open for the light to come through. Quince agrees and then suggests an actor holding a lantern could also represent the moon. But there's another problem: Thisbe and Pyramus are meant to speak through a hole in the wall, so where will they find a wall? Bottom suggests someone plays the Wall so that Thisbe and Pyramus can speak through the Wall's fingers. Quince is satisfied now. He starts the rehearsal, asking anyone not on stage at the time to hide in the bushes until their cue comes.

Robin enters. At first he is afraid that these men are so close to the sleeping Titania, but when he sees they are rehearsing a play he decides to watch, and might join in if the mood takes him. Bottom as Pyramus gets some of his words incorrect—he exchanges "odious" for "odours" and so on. Robin is appalled: he's never seen a stranger Pyramus. As Bottom leaves the stage, Robin follows him. Flute as Thisbe recites all of his lines at once in a rush and even reads the cues!

Robin and Bottom return. Bottom now has a donkey's head instead of his own! Quince and the others run for their lives, afraid of being attacked by this monster. Bottom doesn't understand why they run from him. Robin promises to make Bottom's life a hard one by getting him lost and turning himself into beasts to frighten Bottom with. Snout returns and asks him what he has on his head, then leaves. Quince returns to to bless him and leaves too.

Bottom is suspicious. He thinks they're trying to frighten him into making a fool of himself, but he'll refuse to do such a thing. He'll even sing a song to prove to them that he's not afraid. Titania wakes up. Once Bottom stops singing, Titania begs him to sing again. She loves to look at him, and even though this is the first time she's seen him, she can't help but tell Bottom she loves him. Bottom doesn't see much reason for her to love him, but then he's sure that love and reason don't certainly have much to do with one another anyway. Titania tells him that he is as wise as he is beautiful. Bottom disagrees. If he were exceedingly wise, he'd be out of the woods already. Titania tells him that he can't leave—she won't let him. She loves him. She and her fairy servants will serve him, and give him immortality. Titania calls for her fairies by name: Peaseblossom, Cobweb, Moth, and Mustardseed.

They enter and ask what Titania would have them do. She asks them to be kind to Bottom, to give him food to eat and light to sleep by, and to use butterfly wings to block moonlight getting in his eyes. Bottom asks for their names and awkwardly introduces himself. For instance, he tells Mustardseed he is sorry that most of his family will have been smeared on beef. Titania tells the fairies to take him away so he can sleep. She believes the moon looks sad: either this is because someone is not being loved, or someone is being forced to love without their will. She wants Bottom brought to her quietly.

Act Three, Scene Two

Oberon wonders if Titania is awake yet, and what she has ended up in love with if she is awake. Robin enters. Oberon demands a report on what mischief he has made. He tells Oberon that Titania is in love with a monster, which he created by putting a donkey's head on the bumbling, stupid one playing Pyramus. His friends ran away and were frightened by everything they came across, even bristles and thorns. Robin led them on as trees and bushes pulled on their hats and sleeves. Then, Titania woke up and fell in love with Bottom. Oberon is mightily pleased.

He asks if Robin put the flower juice on the eyes of the Athenian youth as asked. Robin has, and is positive that he will have seen the girl when they woke up as they slept near one another. Oberon tells him to be quiet as the Athenian is approaching. Robin tells Oberon that it is the same woman, but not the same man he saw.

Demetrius and Hermia enter. He doesn't understand why she is so angry with him when he loves her so much. She's upset that he might have killed Lysander while he was asleep. She doesn't believe he would have left her because he's been so faithful to her, so something must have happened to him. She argues that it is obvious that Demetrius has killed Lysander because he looks so pale and grim. Demetrius argues that he looks pale and grim because she is murdering his spirit with her cruel words. Hermia demands to know what he has done with Lysander. Demetrius assures her he didn't kill Lysander, nor does he think Lysander is even dead. Hermia begs him to tell her Lysander is alright, but Demetrius wouldn't get much out of that. Hermia agrees he won't get far with her: she'll never see Demetrius again, even if she never sees Lysander again. She leaves. Demetrius can't go after her while she's this upset, so he decides to lie down and sleep.

Oberon chastises Robin—he's put the flower juice on the wrong person's eyes! He's undone true love, and made false love true! Robin doesn't care much as he believes it is down to fate for love to be so confusing. Oberon orders him to fly through the woods and find Helena, and bring her to Oberon so he can put a charm on her eyes. Robin leaves.

Oberon smears the flower juice across Demetrius' eyes. He hopes that when he sees the girl he's supposed to love he will remember how he feels. Robin announces that Helena is nearby with Lysander, who is begging her to love him. They decide to watch quietly. Robin is excited to watch two men in love with the same woman; this is one of his favourite predicaments.

Lysander and Helena enter first. Lysander doesn't understand why Helena thinks he's making fun of her because he's crying when he tells her that he loves her. People don't cry when they tease someone! Helena still doesn't believe him, because he's made the same promises to both her and Hermia now, and as they can't both be true promises then they have to be false ones. Lysander assures her he wasn't thinking clearly when he made those promises to her. Helena still doesn't believe he's thinking clearly now as he breaks his promises to Hermia, but Lysander doesn't care. Demetrius loves Hermia and can have her.

Demetrius wakes up and proclaims his love for Helena. He calls her beautiful, comparing her lips to cherries, the pure white snow of the mountain as black next to her pale hand. He wants to kiss her hand as it would make him so happy. Helena is upset that they're both now ganging up on her to pretend they love her. She wants them just to hate her again as she knows they do. If they were real men, they would treat her kindly. Not only are they competing for Hermia's love, they're now competing to mock her. Not a manly thing to do at all!

Lysander asks Demetrius not to be cruel: they all know Demetrius loves Hermia. Lysander gives up all claims and love for her in exchange for Demetrius giving up on his claim for Helena. But, Demetrius doesn't want Hermia; he only wants Helena. His love for Hermia was only temporary. Lysander and Demetrius continue to fight with one another until Hermia arrives. She tells them that, even though its hard to see at night, it's much easier to hear, and this is how she has managed to find Lysander—by following his voice. She asks him why he left her by herself, when surely his love for her would have told him to stay. It is his love for Helena that told him to leave! Lysander doesn't understand why she doesn't know that he hates her. Helena is upset that all three of them are in on the plot to mock her. Helena begs Hermia to remember that they grew up together, and are extremely alike. She asks Hermia to remember their vows of friendship. She also reminds Hermia that it isn't lady-like to do what she is doing.

Hermia is thoroughly confused. It sounds, she says, like Helena is insulting her, not the other way around. Helena pushes her to confess that she sent Lysander and Demetrius to find and praise her beauty and confess their love. It makes no sense for Lysander to have rejected Hermia, so of course Hermia has to be involved somehow. Helena doesn't understand why Hermia hates her so much, when actually she should be pitied for being so unlovable. Hermia still doesn't understand what Helena is talking about. Helena tells her to continue with her little game if she pleases—maybe, she suggests, she should even write a book about it! Helena blames herself for being fought over. She shouldn't have followed them into the woods. Either leaving or dying will solve that problem.

Lysander begs her to stay and listen to him. Hermia tells Lysander not to insult Helena, and Demetrius threatens Lysander to stop. Lysander refuses to listen to either of them because he loves Helena. They argue over who loves her more. They decide to duel with one another to prove who loves Helena more. Hermia tries to pull Lysander back, but he tries to throw her off. Demetrius teases him for not fighting with him and pretending Hermia is holding him back. He calls Lysander a coward. Lysander calls Hermia a thorn and tries to shake her off. Hermia is confused—is he joking? Of course he is, Helena tells her, and so is she. Lysander is ready to fight Demetrius as promised once he has shaken Hermia off. Demetrius teases him once again for not upholding his promises terribly often. Lysander doesn't know what to do to prove his hate for Hermia beyond insults; he won't attack or kill her, if that's what Demetrius wants. Hermia finally realizes that Lysander means what he says. She cries out to God to help her.

Hermia turns on Helena, calling her a snake for stealing her beloved Lysander's heart in the night. Helena, in return, argues that Hermia is still pretending with Lysander and Demetrius. She calls Hermia a "puppet". Hermia interprets that to mean she is short and comes to the conclusion that Helena has shown off her height to the boys to make them like her more than the shorter Hermia. Hermia isn't too short to gouge Helena's eyes out though! Helena turns to the boys once more and begs them to stop Hermia from attacking her.

Helena assures Hermia that she loves her, and the only horrible thing she did to Hermia is tell Demetrius about her elopement with Lysander. And the only reason why she did this was because she loves Demetrius so much. She admits she's been foolish, and will return to Athens. Hermia tells her to go, then, but Helena's "foolish heart" keeps her standing still. Hermia wants clarification just who she's leaving her heart with; Helena answer is, of course, with Demetrius. Lysander and Demetrius assure Helena that they won't let Hermia hurt her. Helena refers to their time at school together, where Hermia was a fierce fighter despite being little. Hermia loses her temper over her height being mentioned again.

Demetrius and Lysander leave to fight one another. Hermia blames the duel on Helena, and tells her to stay where she is, but Helena doesn't trust her not to attack her runs away. Hermia doesn't know what to think anymore and leaves too.

Oberon blames Robin for this mess. He doesn't know if Robin did this on purpose or by accident. Robin assures his King that he made a mistake. Oberon had told him that he'd be able to recognize the Athenian youth by his clothes, which is what he did. Robin finds all of this amusing anyway. Oberon is worried that the two men will start to fight and asks Robin to make the sky overcast and as dark as hell so they won't be able to find one another. Then, he bids Robin to imitate the men and call out to them to keep them moving so they can try to fight and tire themselves out. Eventually they will fall to the ground to go to sleep.

Oberon gives Robin a new flower. He tells Robin to smear the flower juice on Lysander's eyes to undo all the damage that has been caused. When they wake up, the night will seem like a dream, and they can then return to Athens. He'll do the same for Titania if she promises to give him the Indian boy. Robin knows they have to work fast as dawn is approaching, and the ghosts of the people who committed suicide are travelling back to their graveyards after wandering around all night. Oberon reminds Robin that they aren't those kind of spirits and that he loves the sunlight, but agrees that a swift resolution before daylight would be for the best. Oberon leaves.

Lysander and Demetrius enter and exit, trying to find one another and are led around by Robin imitating them both. Eventually, Lysander ends up in a dark space and decides to lie down to rest until the early morning light lets him find Demetrius. Demetrius also lies down, equally exhausted by chasing the fake Lysander around. Helena enters and, wanting to escape her troubles for a while, goes to sleep. Robin knows there should be a fourth. Hermia finally appears, intensely weary and upset. She hopes to find Lysander safe and alive, but can't go any further tonight. She goes to sleep. Robin smears the flower juice on Lysander's eyes and tells them to find the woman they honestly love when they wake up.

Act Four

Act Four, Scene One

While Demetrius and the others still sleep, Titania and Bottom enter with her fairy court. Oberon watches them, hidden from sight. She asks Bottom to sit down so she can place flowers in his hair and rub his cheeks. Bottom asks the fairies to scratch his head and bring him honey. Titania wonders if he'd like to hear some music, or have something distinctive to eat. What Bottom would actually like to do is to sleep. He asks that no one wake him. The fairies leave. Titania puts her arms around Bottom to protect him in sleep, tells Bottom she loves him mightily and goes to sleep.

Robin enters. Oberon tells him that he actually feels sorry for Titania. He met her while she was gathering flowers for Bottom's head and, after arguing with her and insulting her, he asked for the Indian boy, which she gladly agreed to. She sent him over with one of her fairies. Now that Oberon has what he wants, he'll release Titania from the spell, and Robin will take the donkey's head from Bottom. They'll only remember this like an unpleasant dream. Oberon squeezes the flower juice on Titania's eyes.

Titania wakes up, afraid because she had an awful dream that she was married to a donkey. Oberon points to Bottom; Titania is shocked! She doesn't want to look at Bottom's face again. Oberon tells her to be quiet while Robin removes Bottom's donkey head. He asks Titania to get the fairies to play music so the sleeping Athenians will continue to sleep soundly. After removing Bottom's donkey head, Robin tells him to see once again through his own foolish eyes.

Oberon asks Titania to dance with him, and she actually agrees! Now that they're together again, Oberon suggests they should dance together for the Duke at his wedding to bless them and their wedding bed. He's convinced that the other Athenian couples will be married at the same time as the Duke and that everything will once again be joyful.

Robin interrupts—he can hear the morning lark! Oberon and Titania leave to walk slowly towards the part of the Earth that is now dark and to talk about the night's events.

Theseus and Hippolyta enter with their servants and Egeus. A hunting horn blows. Theseus asks someone to find the forest ranger so that Hippolyta can hear the sound of the hunting dogs howling. Hippolyta remembers a time, when she was with Hercules and Cadmus, when one of their dogs cornered a bear. The barking, she assures him, was impressive, and echoed off mountains and trees. Theseus suddenly sees the four sleeping Athenians on the ground. Egeus identifies them all. Theseus assumes they came out to the woods knowing that he and Hippolyta would be there. He then realizes that today is the day Hermia is meant to make her decision. Theseus asks the servants to sound the horns to wake them up. They do, and the four wake from their sleep.

They greet Theseus. He asks Lysander and Demetrius if the world is suddenly so peaceful that two enemies can sleep so close to one another. Lysander admits he doesn't truly know how he got there, but the last thing he remembers was his plan to run away with Hermia. Egeus stops him and asks for Theseus to punish him. Demetrius admits that it was true, and he followed them because the beautiful Helena told him where they were going, and was so in love with him that she followed him into the woods. He doesn't quite know how it happened, but his love for Hermia has disappeared, and his love for Helena, who he was once engaged to, has returned. Now, he will always be true to Helena and love her forever.

Theseus overrules Egeus' wishes: the two couples will be married later on after he and Hippolyta are wed. They give up on hunting as the morning grows late, and decide to go back to Athens to get ready for the weddings. All but the four Athenians leave. Demetrius doesn't understand what happened—the previous night's events seem clear and yet cloudy to him. They all agree. Demetrius wonders if they're still asleep and ask them if they saw the Duke, as well. They did. They decide to follow Theseus back to Athens and talk about their dreams along the way. They leave.

Bottom wakes up. He, too, has had a strange "dream". He realizes he has been left alone. He can't put into words what he has just experienced and plans to ask Quince to put it down in words for him as a song. He'll sing it for the Duke during the intermission or when Thisbe dies in the play.

Act Four, Scene Two

Back in Athens, Quince and the others gather to discuss Bottom's whereabouts. They're sure he's been kidnapped as he did not return to his house. They're upset that the play will be ruined now that their lead is nowhere to be found. Snug arrives to tell them that three couples have been married. They're upset about the wages they would have received for putting on the play.

Bottom enters. They're pleased and amazed to see him. He won't tell them about the wondrous dreams he has had just yet as he wants them to get organized for the play. After he gives out several orders, they gather together and leave.

Act Five

Act Five, Scene One

Theseus, Hippolyta, and Philostrate enter. Hippolyta comments that the four Athenians are saying some strange things. Theseus agrees the story sounds perfectly made up, and that he'll never believe them. He blames the hallucinations on love affecting them all. He tells her that when these people are happy, they have such an imagination that they have to blame it on something otherworldly being the cause. Hippolyta points out that they all experienced the same dream, and it remains consistent, so it could perhaps be true.

Demetrius, Helena, Lysander and Hermia arrive. They all wish one another joy in their marriages. Theseus wants to be entertained and asks Philostrate for a list of the entertainment that has been prepared for them while they wait to go to bed. Theseus rejects a few of the plays and performances, either because they are unsuitable, or because he's already heard them. He finally comes to Thisbe and Pyramus, and cannot understand why the play has been pitched as so many contradictory things—both a comedy and a tragedy? Theseus asks for more details. Philostrate tells him the play isn't worth the bother, and the actors are awful. He laughed when he watched the rehearsal of Pyramus' suicide, rather than cried. Theseus wants to see it. Philostrate warns him against it. Theseus will watch it—he's intrigued by ordinary workmen putting on a play, and wants to see what they can do. Philostrate leaves to fetch them.

Hippolyta isn't so sure she'd like to watch poor people making fools of themselves if they can't act, but Theseus assures her that they will be generous with their thanks. Philostrate enters and announces the Prologue is ready to be delivered. Theseus tells him to come in.

Quince as the Prologue warns the audience that they are not there to entertain them, or make them happy. The audience criticizes him for his grammar, speed of delivery and punctuation. The rest of the players come in. Quince continues with the Prologue, and describes the action of the story: Pyramus and Thisbe talk through the chink in the wall and meet by moonlight. A Lion frightens Thisbe, who drops her cloak. The Lion tears through the cloak with his bloodied mouth. Pyramus finds the bloodied cloak and stabs himself in his grief. Thisbe does the same, leaving both of them dead. Quince asks the others to tell the audience more.

Snout tells the audience he is a wall, but no ordinary wall, for his fingers form a chink that the two lovers can talk through. Both Theseus and Demetrius sarcastically praise Snout for his brilliant delivery as they've never heard a wall speak better. Pyramus played by Bottom comes to the wall and is upset that Thisbe has forgotten their meeting time. He curses the wall that separates his and her father's territory. Theseus jokes that the wall should probably talk back. Bottom disagrees. Thisbe finally turns up, and the two lovers talk through the door. After comparing themselves to famous lovers, and trying to kiss one another through the hole in the wall, they decide to meet at Ninny's tomb. Snout leaves, the wall no longer needed in the story. Theseus joke that they should have stuck around for a while longer as the wall no longer separates them. Hippolyta thinks this is the silliest play she's ever seen, but Theseus tells her to use her imagination to fill in the awful spots.

Snug the Lion appears on stage and courteously explains to the audience that he is not a real Lion. The audience compliment him for various characteristics. The Moon then enters, carrying a lantern and explains he represents the Moon. The audience argue whether he represents the Moon well enough. He reveals he is actually playing the man in the Moon, and the lantern represents the Moon itself. None of the audience is sure how exactly the man could fit into the lantern that stands in for the Moon. The Moon gets angry with the audience and tells them that all they need to know is that he is the man in the Moon, the lantern is the Moon, the thorn bush is his thorn bush and the dog, his dog. Demetrius isn't sure how all of these things can fit into the Moon/lantern, but asks them to go on. While Thisbe is frightened by the Lion, and the Lion tears her cloak, the audience compliments them on various elements.

Bottom as Pyramus delivers his emotional lines over the death of Thisbe and then stabs himself. The Moon leaves and Pyramus dies. The audience wonder how Thisbe will find Pyramus without the Moonlight, but they assume the stars and Pyramus' moaning will show her the way. Hippolyta hopes Thisbe won't cry over Pyramus' death too much as he doesn't genuinely deserve it. Thisbe finds Pyramus, stabs herself and dies. The audience joke that the Lion and the Moon will have to bury them. Demetrius adds that the Wall will help too. Bottom breaks character to tell them that the Wall cannot help as it has been taken down. He asks the audience if they would like to hear the Epilogue. Theseus does, not as he doesn't think that a play, which ends with all the characters dead, needs an apology to the audience in at the end as there is no one left to blame. He calls it a good tragedy and asks the actors to dance for them.

As the bell chimes, Theseus announces that it is time for bed, and they should retire to their chambers. They will continue to celebrate for two more weeks, but, for now, they should go to bed. They all leave.

Robin enters. He talks about the kinds of things that happen when night reappears, including the spirits from the graveyards rising up and roaming once more across the land. He's been sent ahead of the fairies to clean up and make sure no one disturbs the sleeping house. Oberon and Titania enter with their fairies. They sing and dance together to bless the house, the marriages, and their future children. They all leave once again except for Robin.

Robin addresses the audience. He tells them that if the play has offended them in any way, that they should think of it like a dream. That nothing they saw actually happened. And if he needs to, he will make things right once again if given a chance. If he doesn't, then he can be called a liar. If they are still friends, they should applaud. He leaves.

The Life and Times of William Shakespeare

The Times Shakespeare Lived In

The Elizabethan London that William Shakespeare arrived in was much different than it is today. Significantly, the population was much smaller. Today, seven and a half million people live in the area known as Greater London. In Shakespeare's time the population was around 200,000 – this still made it an enormous metropolis for the time period and it was the leading city in Europe.

In the sixteenth century London suffered from an extremely high death rate – more people died in the city than were born. It was only the steady influx of newcomers from other English counties and immigrants from Europe that helped London's population grow. The bubonic plague was still a large factor in death counts in the city – in fact many people fled the urban area when the many epidemics rolled through. Shakespeare himself probably returned at times to Stratford when it was healthier to do so. The life expectancy in London at the time was thirty-five years; this seemingly short life expectancy would be lengthened if one survived childhood – many children did not make it to their fifth birthday.

London was a crowded and dirty place – it is not surprising that disease was rampant. The houses were built close together and the streets were very narrow – in many cases only wide enough for a single cart to navigate. There was no indoor plumbing and it would be another three hundred years before a sanitary way of disposing of sewage was built for the city of London.

Shakespeare was born into a time of religious upheaval. The Catholic Church came under pressure from the second Tudor ruler, Henry VIII, to annual his first marriage to Catherine of Aragon. Upon the death of his brother Arthur and Henry's ascendancy to the heir to the English throne, he had married his brother's widow in 1509. Over the years Catherine had given birth to only one surviving heir – a daughter Mary. Twenty-four years later, Henry asked for a divorce so he could marry the young Anne Boleyn. The Pope refused and in 1534 Henry broke from the Church, establishing the Church of England. The throne went to Henry's son Edward VI in 1547 but upon the boy's death in 1553, his half-sister Mary, daughter of Henry and Catherine, became Queen. She was a devout Catholic, and plunged the country back into a period of dissension and conflict, which included persecution and death for Protestants and the re-establishment of the Roman Catholic Church.

Queen Mary's death changed the religious *status quo* in England once again when Queen Elizabeth I came to the throne in 1558. The Catholic Church was once again banned, and the Church of England resurrected in its stead.

England also faced a turning point in its very political existence during Shakespeare's "lost years", those years before his arrival in London when his little is known about his life. In 1588, after Elizabeth I had condemned her cousin Mary, Queen of Scots, to death for conspiracy Spain decided to attack Britain in retaliation for the Roman Catholic Mary's death. The Catholic powers were increasingly fearful of the Protestant movement and with England's break from the Church of Rome now seemingly the final stroke in their relationship, it looked as though Catholicism itself was under threat. Spain rose of fleet of ships to sail upon England and it was thought to be unbeatable. However several factors led to English victory – strategic mistakes on the Spanish side and poor weather were among them. England emerged triumphant, its confidence strong, and the Church of England firmly entrenched. Queen Elizabeth I, known as "Gloriana" always serves as a backdrop to any story of Shakespeare's life. An interesting development during her reign was the acceleration of literacy in Elizabethan England – by the end of her reign, it stood at 33% (probably for males only) and was one of the highest rates in the world.

Queen Elizabeth's reign ended in 1603, when she died in her sleep at the age of sixty-nine. Her cousin's son, James I of Scotland became England's king. He was devoutly Protestant so there was no change in the official Church, and indeed by the beginning of the 17th century, few English citizens had ever attended a Catholic mass.

James enthusiastically supported drama and in particular, Shakespeare's company. Over the next thirteen years, before William's death, the playwright's company would perform for the King one hundred and eighty seven times. It was the time of Shakepeare's greatest dramatic output.

Much information on the London theatres of the day has been gleaned from the journal and business papers of Philip Henslowe, who owned the Rose and Fortune theatres. For his papers we can extrapolate what life for actors and playwrights would have been like during Shakespeare's time. We also know something of the Fortune Theatre's building – the contract to build it has survived. These records were used to build the copy of the Globe Theatre that stands on the banks of the Thames River today. Other information has come from existing diaries and letters that survived the time – mostly from visitors to the city who found the whole experience interesting enough to record.

Shakepeare's Family

William Shakespeare, the son of John Shakespeare and Mary, née Arden, was born in the village of Stratford-upon-Avon in the English county of Warwickshire. Stratford is northwest of London, situated somewhat south of England's center. Shakespeare was born quite possibly on 23 Apr in 1564 – his baptism in the family's parish church on April 26 suggests this. Children in that day and age were often baptized on the third day after their birth.

William was John and Mary's third known child – and the first to survive infancy. His two older sisters, Joan and Margaret, both died before he was born. Of the five younger children (Gilbert, a second Joan, Anne, Richard, and Edmund) Anne died at the age of eight but William's other siblings lived into adulthood. Only the second Joan was to reach what we would consider a good old age – she died in 1646 at the age of seventy-seven.

William's background on his paternal side was, like most of the English of his day, humble. Earlier relatives were not gentry in the least but simple tenant farmers who worked in the parish of nearby Arden. The meaning of the name Shakespeare has long been shrouded in mystery – the rarity of the surname indicates that it probably originated with one man several hundred years before William's birth. Evidence shows that the first Shakespeare was born somewhere north of Warwickshire. By 1389 an Adam Shakespeare was a tenant farmer at Baddesley Clinton in Warwickshire – unfortunately early parish records were not compelled to be kept until not long before William's time so it is not known for sure if he was a direct ancestor. In 1596 William's father John applied for a family coat of arms, citing that his grandfather had been granted land in northern Warwickshire for service under Henry VII in the War of the Roses. Historians believe this was probably a valid claim, but no records have come to light that prove it.

William was the grandson of Richard Shakespeare, a tenant farmer at Snitterfield in Arden who was not a wealthy man but did leave a will in which he named John Shakespeare as administrator, which would indicate he was the eldest surviving son. By the time of Richard's death in 1560, John had been living at nearby Stratford-upon-Avon since 1550. Records show that John had his first house in Henley Street in Stratford by 1552 and had acquired the house next door and one in Greenhill Street by 1556. John's trade was that of a glove-maker and he also worked as a wool dealer and an animal skin-cutter. He may have also worked as a butcher - it would seem that he was a man who was not afraid of work and had some ambition to better himself.

Around 1557 John Shakespeare married Mary Arden, the daughter of the owner of the Snitterfield estate where his father Richard Shakespeare farmed. Mary was the youngest of the eight daughters of Robert Arden – apparently Robert had a hand in marrying his daughters off and John must have seemed a likely prospect at the time – certainly on the social scale the Ardens would have been higher than the Shakespeares.

On his mother's side at least, William's roots in the area were deep. Just to the north of the River Avon is the village of Arden, from which Mary's family undoubtedly took their name. Surnames were beginning to be "set" about four hundred years before William's birth; it is probable that that branch of the family had been in the area for at least that long.

William's grandfather Robert Arden was a man of some means, at least locally. He owned several estates, including the one where Richard Shakespeare was a tenant farmer. The Ardens were Roman Catholic – England at the time was seesawing between the old Catholic Church and Protestantism.   Although the marriage is not found in a surviving record, it is likely that it took place at Aston Cantlow where Mary's father had been buried in 1556 and the ceremony would have been a Catholic one, as Mary Tudor, who had brought Catholicism back to England as the official church, was on the throne. Not long before William's birth in 1564 Elizabeth I became Queen of England and the country made the final break with Roman Catholicism, and the local parish church became part of the new Church of England.

Shakespeare's Childhood and Education

William Shakespeare's accepted birth date of April 23, 1564 has long been open to dispute, but the month and year are probably correct. There are two reasons April 23rd is the sentimental favorite: it is St. George's Day in England (George is the country's patron saint) and Shakespeare died on the same date fifty-two years later. Baby William was baptized on the 26th of April in the parish church of Stratford-upon-Avon and as infants in Tudor times were traditionally baptized on the third day following their birth, historians have happily settled on the 23rd as his date of birth.

William was the third of eight known children born to John Shakespeare and Mary (Arden) Shakespeare, and the first to survive infancy. In fact young William's first year was overshadowed by the spectre of the Black Death, now known more prosaically as the bubonic plague. About 10% of the residents of Stratford died that year and the Shakespeares' must have felt relief their young family's survival. The plague was to continue to be a problem for England's citizens during the Elizabethan era. William was to lose his younger sister, eight-year-old Anne, to the disease. Quite possibly his older sister Margaret, a one-year-old baby, died of the Black Death as well, as it swept through the area in 1563. The survival of William, as the first born son, and after the deaths of older sisters Joan and Margaret, no doubt gave him a special place in the Shakespeare family.

William's childhood home, in Henley Street, Stratford, is still standing and is a typical Tudor structure with decorative half timber and small windows. In Shakespeare's time the house would have had a thatched roof. Henley Street led out of town and William apparently spent much time as a boy wandering and playing the countryside near at hand. He undoubtedly spoke the local dialect and though his own speech was probably more refined due to his education - and undoubtedly influenced by his mother, who came from a higher social stratum than the Shakespeares – William retained a good "ear" for dialectic speech which is evident in his plays and apparently retained his Warwickshire accent until his death.

William's life as a youngster was rural. His father was a craftsman and a tradesman – a glover and maker of leather goods – and records show that neighbors included a tailor and a haberdasher. But also nearby was a blacksmith – who's trade in those times would have been mostly horses – and shepherds lived nearby. As William rambled around the countryside he would have come into contact with the rural inhabitants of various occupations and he would have been well versed in the area's flora and fauna. It is very likely that he knew all the local fairy stories and tales of ghosts, witches, and hobgoblins, which England's rural denizens of the era were particularly fond of these stories. William's later writings show that he was well acquainted with the terms and practices of the rural pursuits of hunting and fishing – like most of his male contemporaries of the time, the young William probably spent many a happy hour engaged in these activities.

As the son of an alderman, William was entitled to a free education. His father John had become an alderman when William was just a baby – John was appointed to replace another alderman who got himself into trouble with the town council. By 1568 he was elected as an alderman and three years later was chief alderman and deputy to the local bailiff (the town's top magistrate). John was involved in local politics for many years, and although his fortunes and position faltered in later years, his son William was guaranteed the best education Stratford could offer.

William's learning took place at King's New School – which is still operating as a boy's school today. The school was originally granted a charter in 1553 by the learned young King Edward VI – a number of schools were erected in his name. It is thought the school was the last of the King Edward Schools as the adolescent Edward died only nine days after its charter was granted. It was familiarly known as the King's New School, and sometimes shortened even more to New School. Today it is known as King Edward VI School (or K.E.S.) and while no records exist from Shakespeare's time, it is generally accepted that William was a pupil and would have begun his education there around 1570 about the time he turned six years old.

The average school day for the middle class boys of Stratford was not an easy one. Students arrived early in the morning, not long after dawn, and remained in school until 5 PM. Breaks were given for meals. The boys also attended school on Saturdays. Church attendance was part of the school day, and much time was given over to the learning of the classical languages and translating classical texts. The Roman poet Ovid made a strong impression on young William. Classical mythology is evident in William's later works and no doubt their influence can be traced back to those formative days in Stratford's New School.

William probably left school around the age of fifteen. What he did then has not been documented but in the normal course of things, he would have worked for his father, at least for a time. He may have also been a school master – his facility with words and his sharp intellect would have made him a good candidate – but perhaps it was simply not his avocation and as time would prove, writing was. Within a few years, though, William was married. Marriage at eighteen in those days was relatively rare – physical maturation coming later to the young of that era compared to today. William, however, had been courting an older woman, and as nature took its course, Anne Hathaway became pregnant. Pregnant brides were common among the rural population – in fact many believed that fertility should be proven before heading for the altar! William Shakespeare and Anne Hathaway were married by license and as William was under twenty-one, he had to obtain his father's consent to marry. The actual parish where their wedding ceremony took place is not known, though it may have been in Shottery, Anne's home parish.

Shakepeare's Adulthood

By the time William Shakespeare was twenty-one years old, he had become the father of three children. His wife Anne gave birth to daughter Susanna in May 1583 and to twins Judith and Hamnet early in 1785. William does appear in an existing legal record for Stratford concerning property owned by his parents in 1786. Unfortunately very little else is on record for the years before he appears in London.

William most likely remained in Stratford for the first few years of his marriage and his knowledge of leather indicates that he probably worked with his glove-making father after he left school. The story that he had been a school master or tutor has long been conjectured. A story of William teaching in a more the Catholic-friendly county of Lancashire has been bandied about. None of the stories have any real evidence to back them up, however.

William and Anne lived in the house on Henley Street with his parents. It is hard to conceive that he would have deserted his wife and children when the latter were so young – William came from a comfortable solidly middle class family and he would have likely been taught to fulfill his responsibilities. Shakespeare may have spent his working career in London, and hints of philandering came forth, but he always remained faithful to Stratford and returned often and in middle age, he returned for good. How happy or unhappy he and Anne were together is simply not known. The fact that no children were born to Anne after the twins arrived may speak volumes – but it may also simply be that the birth of twins rendered her unable to have more children. That William did send home much of his acquired wealth in London does at least indicate that he had not entirely deserted his family responsibilities – but whether it was done out of love or duty, we do not have any way of knowing. The years between 1585 and 1592 are considered Shakespeare's "lost years". Simply put, there is no hard evidence of what William was doing during those years.

We also know little about William's wife Anne – she was one of seven children of Richard Hathaway, a yeoman farmer. She was left a small sum of money in his will when he died the year before her marriage and she was to come into this inheritance upon her marriage. The house she grew up in, known as Anne Hathaway's Cottage, is now open to the public, but is more than a mere cottage, having twelve rooms. It is about a mile from the center of Stratford. Anne's gravestone is still in existence as well, and from it her approximate date of birth is calculated – it records that she died in 1623, aged sixty-seven. No verified portraits of her exist and there is no known written description of what she looked like. Some Shakespearean experts believe that Sonnet 145 was written for Anne – the sonnet only really makes sense when the reader understands the wordplay with "hate" and "away" – close enough to mimic her surname, Hathaway.

What were William's influences before he arrived in London to make his way in the world of drama? Certainly he had enjoyed a classical education as a lad and some historians that theorized that he was somehow exposed to more in his late teens and twenties – even if only as a schoolmaster. As for the world of the stage, despite Shakespeare living in a somewhat isolated and rural area, it was quite common for bands of actors to be traveling the countryside plying their trade. These plague haunted years drove many people out of London and into the healthier countryside and actors had to make a living too. They were not above staging performances wherever they could gather enough people to pay the entrance fee. Actors were usually required to have a patron and many wore a badge that identified him as such – this kept the local authorities from looking upon actors as a liability to their parishes. The companies were often sponsored by men of means and even by the nobility. The first acting company created in the reign of Queen Elizabeth I (who came to the throne in 1558) was Lord Leicester's Men in 1574 – the Earls of Sussex and Oxford also had companies by 1582. There was rivalry between the companies and apparently, the Lord Mayor of London disliked the acting groups intensely. Unfortunately, few records for the acting companies have survived.

At least one acting company, The Queen's Men, put in more than one appearance at Stratford in 1589 – and if William was still living there, he very well could have attended their performances. Again, precisely why Shakespeare went to London is not known – but he may have simply been seduced by the theatre life and combined with his love of words it would have seemed the perfect home for him. Again, conjecture comes into deciding Shakespeare's life (one theory has it that William had clung to the old Catholic ways and went to northern England where there was more toleration) but his reasons for going to London remain a mystery. Fortunately for the literary world, he *was* drawn to the theatre and left a stunning literary legacy.

What did William do once he reached London? Again, we don't know for sure, as there are few employment records that have survived from centuries past. Shakespeare did appear in the London in the late 1580's and if he was immediately attracted to the theatre, he would have headed to Southwark, on the south side of the Thames, where many of the restrictions of the city of London did not apply. The entertainment industry of its day was free to do as they wanted there. A tradition has survived down through the centuries that William first got a job holding horses outside the theatre and then moved up to be a prompter's assistant. It is known that within a few years William was "becoming Shakespeare" and was writing.

With so many blanks to fill in his life and so very little solid evidence of Shakespeare's very existence at this point, how is it known that he was writing by 1592? It is thanks to one Robert Greene, another London writer. Greene published an attack on William, accusing him of plagiarism and calling him an "upstart crow". Greene parodied some lines from the history play *Henry VI Part III* and intimated that Shakespeare was stealing from his competition. Greene died soon after this, but the publisher of the attack apologized in print – which indicates that William, still a young man at twenty-eight, had enough of a reputation or at least enough gall, to demand a retraction.

If *Henry VI Part III* had already been written by 1592, there is a good chance that Parts I and II had already been penned as well. This accomplishment would have been remarkable for such a young man, and one who had not attended university as well. His lack of higher education seemed to be an issue with some of his contemporary writers – snobbism not being exclusive to the modern world. Fellow writers, who looked at Shakespeare critically and no doubt enviously, included Christopher Marlowe and Thomas Nashe.

Henry VI Part III was not William's first play. *The Two Gentlemen of Verona* was written sometime between 1588 and 1590. Although it is difficult to determine exactly when many of his early plays were written, it is thought that *A Comedy of Errors* might have been his first comedic play and could have been written as early as 1591. In 1594, Shakespeare created Titus Andronicus, his first attempt at tragedy.

There is nothing in the scant surviving records to suggest that William worked for a theatrical company during his early years in London. It is very likely he worked as a freelance writer, as many of contemporaries of the time did. Looking again at his private life, it is possible that during his early years he was returning home to Stratford at regular intervals.

It is thought that during his early years, he worked with other writers to produce collaborative works. *Sir*

Thomas More, a historical play about the martyred Thomas More who was executed by Henry VIII, was co-written with Anthony Munday and Henry Chettle, the latter being the very publisher who retracted Robert Greene's accusation of plagiarism in 1592. Experts believe this was written during Shakespeare's early period.

It is known that it didn't take long for William's work to attract the interest of several different theatrical companies. *Titus Andronicus* was first performed by Sussex's Men. Pembroke's Men also performed several of William's plays and at least two known performance venues are on record – The Inns of Court and the Bankside Rose playhouse. Some Shakespearean historians believe that William had joined the Queen's Men on tour before he arrived in London – some of his later plays are similar to plays they performed in the mid 1580's.

The theatres of London were not a stable entity in the 1590's. Once again, the pall of the plague hung over the city in the summer of 1592. The Puritans, a Protestant faction that had gained some power in the Elizabethan era, despised what they saw as the licentiousness of theatre life and pressured the city to shut down acting venues in London and Southwark. They blamed the theatres for spreading the Plague. The theatres remained closed for two years.

Whether William remained in London for the duration of the Plague years is unknown, but it is known that he turned to writing poetry. In 1593 the rather racy poem *Venus and Adonis* appeared and was dedicated to Henry Wriothesley, the Earl of Southampton. The Earl was a patron of the arts – he supported several poets and often attended the theatre. Shakespeare may have looked upon him as opportunity knocking; after all, having a patron was easier that freelancing. It has been conjectured that Shakespeare's poems were written to Wriothesley as expressions of love and passion; many have conjectured that Shakespeare had homosexual or bisexual leanings. This could be or it might just be that Shakespeare saw an opportunity and wrote what Wriothesley wanted. Without solid evidence, it is impossible to know.

Shakespeare also dedicated the more serious and tragic poem *The Rape of Lucrece* to Wriothesley in 1594. It was about a Roman married woman who is raped by a Roman prince – she then commits suicide. The Rape of Lucrece was not quite as successful as Venus and Adonis but by now Shakespeare's reputation as a writer was established.

William returned to play writing once the Plague had died down again by the fall of 1594. A new theatrical company was formed by Lord Hunsdon (who was Queen Elizabeth's Lord Chamberlain), and called the Chamberlain's Men. Evidence has survived that indicate that Shakespeare was part of the company. Richard Burbage was also part of Chamberlain's Men – he became the company's star actor and would be the lead in many of the Shakespeare plays that they performed. Many of the actors who belonged to the company also had a financial stake in it.

The Chamberlain's Men did well from the start. They first performed for theatre-owner Philip Henslowe in 1594 and were on the bill at Court later that year over the Christmas season. The Chamberlain's Men main rival in London's theatre world was the Admiral's Men and between the two of them, they put on all theatrical performances in the city.

Lord Chamberlain's Men now had a base at the Shoreditch Theatre on the London side of the Thames River. This was an important factor for the rest of William's career – it now settled down to something of permanence. Shakespeare was an asset to the company – he brought in his body of work that could serve as part of the company's repertoire for years to come. William produced about two plays a year until he left London to live out his final days in Stratford.

The first Shakespeare play that was a success after the Plague years was *Richard III*, another history play that chronicled the downfall of the Plantagenet royal house and opened the door for the rise of the Tudor dynasty. No doubt this play was popularly supported by the monarch and her Court of the time. Three other well-regarded and often performed plays were thought to have been written during William's first years with the Chamberlain's Men – *A Midsummer Night's Dream*, *Romeo and Juliet*, *Love's Labour Lost*, and *Richard II*. The variety of comedy, tragedy, and history plays reflect Shakespeare's talent and versatility. Around this time Shakespeare garnered high praise from a fellow writer Francis Meres. Meres made reference to William's sonnets, which were not actually published for another eleven years.

Tragedy struck the Shakespeare family in 1596 when William and Anne's only son Hamnet. In 1597 William, obviously enjoying some material success with his writing career, purchased a larger house in Stratford, New Place, the second largest estate in the parish. Shakespeare still spent much of his time in London but as the years went on, he returned to Stratford more and more. The playwright was not only a creative type – he had a keen business sense, as well, or possibly good advisors. He invested in property, and by 1599 he was part owner of the Globe Theatre, forever afterward associated with Shakespeare.

After the Globe Theatre was built in 1599 Shakespeare became a prominent member of the King's Men – the company was sponsored by the King himself, James I, when he ascended the throne in 1603. The company was commanded to produce and perform plays "for our (the King's) solace and pleasure". Shakespeare produced a great body of work over the next ten years. The Globe burned down during a performance of Henry VIII (a fired canon caused the thatched roof to catch fire). No one was killed, and the Globe was rebuilt soon after. At about this time, after investing in the new theatre, Shakespeare retired to spend most of his time in Stratford. He died at New Place on his 52nd birthday. He was survived by his wife, two daughters, two sons-in-law, and a grandchild. His wife Anne outlived him, dying in 1623. One of the few official documentation of Shakepeare's to have survived is his will – in which he left his wife "his second-best bed" (by law, she would have also inherited one-third of his estate). William and Anne were survived by their two daughters, both married and who would leave descendants.

Modern Version of the Play

Act 1

Scene I

The palace of THESEUS.

Enter THESEUS, HIPPOLYTA, PHILOSTRATE, and Attendants

THESEUS

Now, fair Hippolyta, our nuptial hour

My dear Hippolyta, our wedding day

Draws on apace; four happy days bring in

Is coming soon, in exactly four days, when there is

Another moon: but, O, methinks, how slow

a new moon: but too slowly

This old moon wanes! she lingers my desires,

is this moon waning! It is making me wait anxiously,

Like to a step-dame or a dowager

Like a step-mother or a widow

Long withering out a young man revenue.

makes a son wait for his inheritance.

HIPPOLYTA

Four days will quickly steep themselves in night;

But four days will quickly become four nights,

Four nights will quickly dream away the time;

And we will dream through the four nights,

And then the moon, like to a silver bow

And then the new moon, shaped like a silver bow

New-bent in heaven, shall behold the night

Pulled back in the sky, will look at the night

Of our solemnities.

That marks the day of our marriage.

THESEUS

Go, Philostrate,

Go, Philostrate,

Stir up the Athenian youth to merriments;

And get the young people of Athens to party.

Awake the pert and nimble spirit of mirth;

Wake up the city with an air of celebration

Turn melancholy forth to funerals;

And allow sadness only for funerals –

The pale companion is not for our pomp.

We do not need it mixed with our joy and festivities.

Exit PHILOSTRATE

Hippolyta, I woo'd thee with my sword,

Hippolyta, I courted you by sword in battle

And won thy love, doing thee injuries;

And won your love as I defeated and kidnapped you –

But I will wed thee in another key,

But our wedding will be different,

With pomp, with triumph and with revelling.

celebratory, triumphant, and joyful.

Enter EGEUS, HERMIA, LYSANDER, and DEMETRIUS

EGEUS

Happy be Theseus, our renowned duke!

I hope you are well, Duke Theseus!

THESEUS

Thanks, good Egeus: what's the news with thee?

Thank you, Egeus

EGEUS

Full of vexation come I, with complaint

I am confused and worried for

Against my child, my daughter Hermia.

Hermia, my daughter and child.

Stand forth, Demetrius. My noble lord,

Come forward, Demetrius. My Lord,

This man hath my consent to marry her.

I have agreed to this man marrying her.

Stand forth, Lysander: and my gracious duke,

Come forward, Lysander: and good duke,

This man hath bewitch'd the bosom of my child;

This man has tricked my daughter's heart.

Thou, thou, Lysander, thou hast given her rhymes,

You, Lysander, you have written her poems,

And interchanged love-tokens with my child:

And given her trinkets and gifts:

Thou hast by moonlight at her window sung,

At night, below her window, you sang to her,

With feigning voice verses of feigning love,

Deceiving her with insincere lyrics of untrue love,

And stolen the impression of her fantasy

And have stirred her imagination

With bracelets of thy hair, rings, gawds, conceits,

With locks of hair, rings, toys, favors,

Knacks, trifles, nosegays, sweetmeats, messengers

Knickknacks, charms, flowers, and desserts, convincing

Of strong prevailment in unharden'd youth:

Signs to strongly sway a naive youth.

With cunning hast thou filch'd my daughter's heart,

Sneakily you have stolen my daughter's love,

Turn'd her obedience, which is due to me,

So that she obeys you instead of me, and to me

To stubborn harshness: and, my gracious duke,

Acts stubbornly and rudely. And now, gracious duke,

Be it so she; will not here before your grace

I ask that you let me, if she will not here

Consent to marry with Demetrius,

Agree to marrying Demetrius,

I beg the ancient privilege of Athens,

Do what I am allowed as an Athenian father,

As she is mine, I may dispose of her:

Who owns his daughter, and send her away:

Which shall be either to this gentleman

Either to marry Demetrius,

Or to her death, according to our law

Or to die, according to the law.

Immediately provided in that case.

THESEUS

What say you, Hermia? be advised fair maid:

Well, Hermia – how do you respond? Know this:

To you your father should be as a god;

Your father should be thought of as your god –

One that composed your beauties, yea, and one

He created you, as beautiful as you are, and

To whom you are but as a form in wax

So you are only a wax model

By him imprinted and within his power

That he has signed as the artist, and as such

To leave the figure or disfigure it.

He may leave it untouched, or demolish it.

Demetrius is a worthy gentleman.

Demetrius is well worth marrying.

HERMIA

So is Lysander.

But Lysander is as well.

THESEUS

In himself he is;

Yes, outside of this situation he is,

But in this kind, wanting your father's voice,

But considering your father's opinion

The other must be held the worthier.

Demetrius is the better man.

HERMIA

I would my father look'd but with my eyes.

I wish my father could see this as I do!

THESEUS

Rather your eyes must with his judgment look.

No, you should instead see it as he does.

HERMIA

I do entreat your grace to pardon me.

Please forgive me for what I am going to say.

I know not by what power I am made bold,

I do not know how I feel so confident to speak honestly,

Nor how it may concern my modesty,

or how much I am overstepping my place and being ill-mannered,

In such a presence here to plead my thoughts;

And bring my case to you who are my authority;

But I beseech your grace that I may know

But I ask, because I wish to know for sure,

The worst that may befall me in this case,

What is the worst that might happen to me

If I refuse to wed Demetrius.

If I refuse to marry Demetrius?

THESEUS

Either to die the death or to abjure

You must either die or be banished

For ever the society of men.

From marrying and sent to a nunnery.

Therefore, fair Hermia, question your desires;

So, beautiful Hermia, step back and search yourself,

Know of your youth, examine well your blood,

Understand your immaturity, your youth, and your temperament,

Whether, if you yield not to your father's choice,

So you can know, if you do not obey your father,

You can endure the livery of a nun,

If you can live the rest of your life as a nun.

For aye to be in shady cloister mew'd,

You would be caged in a dark convent

To live a barren sister all your life,

All your life, living as a nun, childless,

Chanting faint hymns to the cold fruitless moon.

Chanting hymns to the cold moon, which like you is without child.

Thrice-blessed they that master so their blood,

Believe me, those that can quell their desires are blessed triple

To undergo such maiden pilgrimage;

For journeying through life as a nun is admirable –

But earthlier happy is the rose distill'd,

But on this earth, it is happier to be married, like a rose perfume,

Than that which withering on the virgin thorn

Rather than the rose that on the same stem

Grows, lives and dies in single blessedness.

Grows, lives, and dies, alone but chaste and blessed.

HERMIA

So will I grow, so live, so die, my lord,

So I will likewise grow, live, and die alone, my lord

Ere I will my virgin patent up

Before I consent to losing my virginity

Unto his lordship, whose unwished yoke

To Demetrius, whose bond of marriage I do not wish

My soul consents not to give sovereignty.

And to whose authority my soul does not desire to bow.

THESEUS

Take time to pause; and, by the nest new moon--

Take time and think about your decision until the new moon –

The sealing-day betwixt my love and me,

– which is when Hippolyta and I will marry

For everlasting bond of fellowship--

and be forever joined together –

Upon that day either prepare to die

And then you must be ready to die

For disobedience to your father's will,

For disobeying your father's will,

Or else to wed Demetrius, as he would;

Or ready to wed Demetrius, as your father wishes,

Or on Diana's altar to protest

Or like the chaste Roman goddess Diana, commit

For aye austerity and single life.

Yourself to the nun's vows of lifelong celibacy.

DEMETRIUS

Relent, sweet Hermia: and, Lysander, yield

Change your mind, sweet Hermia! And Lysander, give up

Thy crazed title to my certain right.

Your claim to the woman I am due to marry.

LYSANDER

You have her father's love, Demetrius;

Demetrius, you can have her father's love

Let me have Hermia's: do you marry him.

And I can have Hermia's — why don't you marry him?

EGEUS

Scornful Lysander! true, he hath my love,

Rude Lysander! Yes, I love Demetrius,

And what is mine my love shall render him.

And so I will give him what is mine:

And she is mine, and all my right of her

My daughter, and the right to marry her

I do estate unto Demetrius.

Is so allowed to Demetrius.

LYSANDER

I am, my lord, as well derived as he,

You know, sir, I come from as good a family as he does,

As well possess'd; my love is more than his;

I am just as rich, and I love Hermia more.

My fortunes every way as fairly rank'd,

In everything I rank just as highly,

If not with vantage, as Demetrius';

If not higher, than Demetrius,

And, which is more than all these boasts can be,

And moreover, which should be what is most important,

I am beloved of beauteous Hermia:

Beautiful Hermia loves me in return:

Why should not I then prosecute my right?

Why should I not be able to marry her?

Demetrius, I'll avouch it to his head,

Demetrius, I promise this is true,

Made love to Nedar's daughter, Helena,

Wooed Nedar's daughter, Helena,

And won her soul; and she, sweet lady, dotes,

Until she fell for him, and she, poor girl, loves,

Devoutly dotes, dotes in idolatry,

Loves deeply, almost to the point of obsession,

Upon this spotted and inconstant man.

This flawed and inconsistent man.

THESEUS

I must confess that I have heard so much,

Admittedly, I have heard similar rumors

And with Demetrius thought to have spoke thereof;

And even considered speaking directly to Demetrius about them,

But, being over-full of self-affairs,

But, being so busy with my own obligations

My mind did lose it. But, Demetrius, come;

Forgot about it. Demetrius, come with me,

And come, Egeus; you shall go with me,

And you, Egeus, come with me as well:

I have some private schooling for you both.

I have some words in private to share with you both.

For you, fair Hermia, look you arm yourself

As for you, Hermia, prepare yourself

To fit your fancies to your father's will;

To do whatever your father's will commands,

Or else the law of Athens yields you up--

Or else you must go before the Athenian Law –

Which by no means we may extenuate--

From which we cannot save you –

To death, or to a vow of single life.

And either die or become a nun.

Come, my Hippolyta: what cheer, my love?

Come, Hippolyta – how are you, my love?

Demetrius and Egeus, go along:

Demetrius and Egeus, come with us.

I must employ you in some business

I must as you about something

Against our nuptial and confer with you

Regarding my wedding, and speak with you

Of something nearly that concerns yourselves.

About something that concerns both of you.

EGEUS

With duty and desire we follow you.

We follow in order to obey, and because we want to hear your words.

Exeunt all but LYSANDER and HERMIA

LYSANDER

How now, my love! why is your cheek so pale?

Oh Hermia, what is wrong? Why are you pale?

How chance the roses there do fade so fast?

How did the rosy redness of your cheeks fade away so quickly?

HERMIA

Belike for want of rain, which I could well

Like roses, my cheeks need rain, which I could

Beteem them from the tempest of my eyes.

Give them by crying a storm upon them.

LYSANDER

Ay me! for aught that I could ever read,

Oh no! But listen: everything I have read,

Could ever hear by tale or history,

Either in fairy tale or true history,

The course of true love never did run smooth;

Says true love must always overcome problems:

But, either it was different in blood,--

Sometimes the problem is being from different classes--

HERMIA

O cross! too high to be enthrall'd to low.

How horrible to be so wealthy and in love with someone so poor!

LYSANDER

Or else misgraffed in respect of years,--

And sometimes there was a great age difference--

HERMIA

O spite! too old to be engaged to young.

How awful to be so old and marrying someone so young!

LYSANDER

Or else it stood upon the choice of friends,--

And sometimes the lovers' friends were against the match--

HERMIA

O hell! to choose love by another's eyes.

How hellish to have to love only whom someone else chose!

LYSANDER

Or, if there were a sympathy in choice,

And sometimes, if the match was a good one,

War, death, or sickness did lay siege to it,

War or death or illness attacked it

Making it momentary as a sound,

And ended it, as transient as a sound becoming silent,

Swift as a shadow, short as any dream;

As quick as a shadow disappearing, as short as a dream upon waking,

Brief as the lightning in the collied night,

As brief as a lightning strike in the black night sky

That, in a spleen, unfolds both heaven and earth,

That at once shows the earth and the sky

And ere a man hath power to say 'Behold!'

And, before a man can say "Look!"

The jaws of darkness do devour it up:

Is gone into darkness, as if swallowed.

So quick bright things come to confusion.

Thus, good and bright things may quickly change.

HERMIA

If then true lovers have been ever cross'd,

Then it seems that true lovers are so often troubled

It stands as an edict in destiny:

66

That fighting obstacles is their fate.

Then let us teach our trial patience,

So we should be patient in this trial

Because it is a customary cross,

Because it is just as normal of a problem

As due to love as thoughts and dreams and sighs,

For lovers as thoughts, dreams, sighs

Wishes and tears, poor fancy's followers.

Wishes, and tears – all things that accompany love.

LYSANDER

A good persuasion: therefore, hear me, Hermia.

I agree, Hermia, now listen:

I have a widow aunt, a dowager

I have a widowed aunt

Of great revenue, and she hath no child:

Who is very wealthy and has no child for her inheritance.

From Athens is her house remote seven leagues;

She lives far from Athens

And she respects me as her only son.

And loves me like a son.

There, gentle Hermia, may I marry thee;

We should thus, gentle Hermia, go there to wed,

And to that place the sharp Athenian law

Because that far away the Athenian Law

Cannot pursue us. If thou lovest me then,

Has no effect. So, if you love me,

Steal forth thy father's house to-morrow night;

Run away from your father's house tomorrow night

And in the wood, a league without the town,

And go to the forest, a mile outside of town,

Where I did meet thee once with Helena,

To the place where I once met Helena

To do observance to a morn of May,

And watched the sunrise one May:

There will I stay for thee.

I will wait for you there.

HERMIA

My good Lysander!

Oh good Lysander!

I swear to thee, by Cupid's strongest bow,

I promise, by the bow of Cupid, messenger of Love,

By his best arrow with the golden head,

By his best arrow with a golden tip,

By the simplicity of Venus' doves,

By Venus' doves which are simple and pure,

By that which knitteth souls and prospers loves,

By the fates that tie lovers together and gives them success,

And by that fire which burn'd the Carthage queen,

And by the fire that the Carthage queen burned herself in

When the false Troyan under sail was seen,

When her lover from Troy left by the sea,

By all the vows that ever men have broke,

By all the promises that men have broken

In number more than ever women spoke,

Which far outnumber the promises women made,

In that same place thou hast appointed me,

In the place that you have told me to go

To-morrow truly will I meet with thee.

Will I be, tomorrow, to see you.

LYSANDER

Keep promise, love. Look, here comes Helena.

Keep your word, love. Look, here comes Helena.

Enter HELENA

HERMIA

God speed fair Helena! whither away?

Greetings beautiful Helena! Where are you going?

HELENA

Call you me fair? that fair again unsay.

You call me beautiful? Well don't:

Demetrius loves your fair: O happy fair!

Demetrius prefers your beauty – oh, that is the best beauty!

Your eyes are lode-stars; and your tongue's sweet air

Your eyes are like bright stars and your voice

More tuneable than lark to shepherd's ear,

Is more pleasing than the songbird is to the shepherd

When wheat is green, when hawthorn buds appear.

In Springtime when the wheat is still green and the flower buds first appear.

Sickness is catching: O, were favour so,

I feel sick: if only a lover's preference were like sickness,

Yours would I catch, fair Hermia, ere I go;

Then I could catch Demetrius's favor from you, fair Helena, before I leave.

My ear should catch your voice, my eye your eye,

Your voice would infect my ear and my eyes would become as yours,

My tongue should catch your tongue's sweet melody.

My voice as sweet and melodious as your voice.

Were the world mine, Demetrius being bated,

Were everything in the world mine except Demetrius,

The rest I'd give to be to you translated.

I would give it to you just to be changed into you.

O, teach me how you look, and with what art

Teach me how you create your beauty and how

You sway the motion of Demetrius' heart.

You captured Demetrius's eye and favor.

HERMIA

I frown upon him, yet he loves me still.

I never smile at him, I only frown, but it has no effect: he loves me still.

HELENA

O that your frowns would teach my smiles such skill!

I wish I could teach my smiles how to be as alluring as your frowns!

HERMIA

I give him curses, yet he gives me love.

I am rude to him and curse him, and he responds in love.

HELENA

O that my prayers could such affection move!

I wish my prayers and well-wishing could be as powerful!

HERMIA

The more I hate, the more he follows me.

I hate him more and more, and all it does is make him follow me more.

HELENA

The more I love, the more he hateth me.

And the more I love him, the more he hates me.

HERMIA

His folly, Helena, is no fault of mine.

I have done nothing to warrant his silly feelings for me.

HELENA

None, but your beauty: would that fault were mine!

No, but your beauty has done enough: I wish I had that problem.

HERMIA

Take comfort: he no more shall see my face;

Don't worry, he will not see me anymore

Lysander and myself will fly this place.

After Lysander and I run away.

Before the time I did Lysander see,

Before I met Lysander,

Seem'd Athens as a paradise to me:

Athens was my paradise:

O, then, what graces in my love do dwell,

But Lysander is so wonderful

That he hath turn'd a heaven unto a hell!

That in comparison this heaven is more like a hell!

LYSANDER

Helen, to you our minds we will unfold:

Helen, we will tell you our secret:

To-morrow night, when Phoebe doth behold

Tomorrow night, when the moon looks down,

Her silver visage in the watery glass,

Like a silver eye, on a lake,

Decking with liquid pearl the bladed grass,

Coloring each blade of grass silver,

A time that lovers' flights doth still conceal,

A time late at night that hides lovers' plans from those asleep,

Through Athens' gates have we devised to steal.

We have planned to leave Athens.

HERMIA

And in the wood, where often you and I

And in the forest where we used to

Upon faint primrose-beds were wont to lie,

Lie on the flower beds

Emptying our bosoms of their counsel sweet,

And talk about everything on our minds,

There my Lysander and myself shall meet;

That is where Lysander and I will meet.

And thence from Athens turn away our eyes,

From then, we will no longer look at Athens

To seek new friends and stranger companies.

And instead seek out new friends and communities.

Farewell, sweet playfellow: pray thou for us;

Goodbye my friend! Pray for us

And good luck grant thee thy Demetrius!

And we wish you good luck with Demetrius!

Keep word, Lysander: we must starve our sight

Be faithful, Lysander. Now we must not

From lovers' food till morrow deep midnight.

See each otehr until late tomorrow night.

LYSANDER

I will, my Hermia.

Exit HERMIA

Helena, adieu:

Goodbye, Helena:

As you on him, Demetrius dote on you!

I hope Demetrius returns the love you give to him!

Exit

HELENA

How happy some o'er other some can be!

Some are so much happier than others!

Through Athens I am thought as fair as she.

In Athens, many think me as beautiful as Hermia,

But what of that? Demetrius thinks not so;

But what does that mean since Demetrius does not?

He will not know what all but he do know:

He does not accept what everyone else seems to agree on

And as he errs, doting on Hermia's eyes,

And while he mistakenly obsesses over Hermia's eyes

So I, admiring of his qualities:

So too I am mistaken in admiring him.

Things base and vile, folding no quantity,

Evil and disgusting qualities

Love can transpose to form and dignity:

Are transformed by love to fair and noble things.

Love looks not with the eyes, but with the mind;

Love does not look with the same eyes others have, but with one's mind:

And therefore is wing'd Cupid painted blind:

This is why Cupid is painted as being blind

Nor hath Love's mind of any judgement taste;

And why Love does not have good judgement.

Wings and no eyes figure unheedy haste:

With wings and no eyes, Cupid is hasty

And therefore is Love said to be a child,

And so Love is like a child

Because in choice he is so oft beguiled.

Making bad and reckless choices.

As waggish boys in game themselves forswear,

As playful boys jokingly lie,

So the boy Love is perjured every where:

So too does Love lie and break its promises:

For ere Demetrius look'd on Hermia's eyne,

Before Demetrius fell for Hermia's beauty,

He hail'd down oaths that he was only mine;

He swore repeatedly to be true to me,

And when this hail some heat from Hermia felt,

And then when Hermia's presence came into his mind,

So he dissolved, and showers of oaths did melt.

He weakened his vows to me.

I will go tell him of fair Hermia's flight:

I will tell him of Hermia's plan

Then to the wood will he to-morrow night

And tomorrow night he will go to the forest

Pursue her; and for this intelligence

And follow her. Perhaps, after telling him this,

If I have thanks, it is a dear expense:

He will be grateful, and that will make it worthwhile,

But herein mean I to enrich my pain,

Although it will hurt me even more

To have his sight thither and back again.

To see him leave and then return again.

Exit

Scene II
Athens. QUINCE'S house.

Enter QUINCE, SNUG, BOTTOM, FLUTE, SNOUT, and STARVELING

QUINCE

Is all our company here?

Is everyone here?

BOTTOM

You were best to call them generally, man by man,

It would be easier to take attendance individually

according to the scrip.

by a roll-call.

QUINCE

Here is the scroll of every man's name, which is

Here is the list of the actors

thought fit, through all Athens, to play in our

that all of Athens considers talented and are able to perform

interlude before the duke and the duchess, on his

in our skit for the duke and duchess

wedding-day at night.

at their wedding.

BOTTOM

First, good Peter Quince, say what the play treats

Peter Quince, you should first explain what the play is about,

on, then read the names of the actors, and so grow

and then read the cast,

to a point.

for clarity's sake.

QUINCE

Marry, our play is, The most lamentable comedy, and

Of course: we will perform "The Sad Comedy and

most cruel death of Pyramus and Thisby.

Cruel Death of Pyramus and Thisby."

BOTTOM

A very good piece of work, I assure you, and a

A very good play, I promise, and

merry. Now, good Peter Quince, call forth your

fun. Now, Peter Quince, call out

actors by the scroll. Masters, spread yourselves.

the actors. Everyone, spread out so you can hear.

QUINCE

Answer as I call you. Nick Bottom, the weaver.

Respond when I call you. Nick Bottom, the weaver.

BOTTOM

Ready. Name what part I am for, and proceed.

I'm here. Who am I playing?

QUINCE

You, Nick Bottom, are set down for Pyramus.

You will play Pyramus.

BOTTOM

What is Pyramus? a lover, or a tyrant?

And who is he? A lover, a villain?

QUINCE

A lover, that kills himself most gallant for love.

A lover who nobly kills himself for love.

BOTTOM

That will ask some tears in the true performing of

It sounds like I will have to cry in order to perform it well.

it: if I do it, let the audience look to their

If so, the audience should prepare themselves:

eyes; I will move storms, I will condole in some

I will cause storms and strongly emote my grief.

measure. To the rest: yet my chief humour is for a

Now continue– but you know I play

tyrant: I could play Ercles rarely, or a part to

the tyrant best. I would make a good Hercules, or any part

tear a cat in, to make all split.

where I could yell and shout angrily, listen:

The raging rocks

And shivering shocks

Shall break the locks

Of prison gates;

And Phibbus' car

Shall shine from far

And make and mar

The foolish Fates.

This was lofty! Now name the rest of the players.

How great was that! Now continue with the other actors—

This is Ercles' vein, a tyrant's vein; a lover is

so you know, that was Hercules as a tyrant. My lover part

more condoling.

will be much sadder.

QUINCE

Francis Flute, the bellows-mender.

Francis Flute, who repairs bellows.

FLUTE

Here, Peter Quince.

Here, Peter Quince.

QUINCE

Flute, you must take Thisby on you.

Flute, you will play Thisby.

FLUTE

What is Thisby? a wandering knight?

And who is Thisby? A knight on a quest?

QUINCE

It is the lady that Pyramus must love.

Thisby is the lady Pyramus loves.

FLUTE

Nay, faith, let me not play a woman; I have a beard coming.

No, please, do not make me play a woman. I have a beard coming in.

QUINCE

That's all one: you shall play it in a mask, and

That doesn't matter – you will play it in a mask

you may speak as small as you will.

and you can make your voice high and disguised.

BOTTOM

An I may hide my face, let me play Thisby too, I'll

If Thisby requires a mask, let me play both!

speak in a monstrous little voice. 'Thisne,

I'll speak in a little voice after playing Pyramus, saying,

Thisne;' 'Ah, Pyramus, lover dear! thy Thisby dear,

"Thisne! Thisne!" and then as Thisby, "Pyramus my love! I am here,

and lady dear!'

your dear lady!"

QUINCE

No, no; you must play Pyramus: and, Flute, you Thisby.

No – you will be Pyramus, and Flute will be Thisby.

BOTTOM

Well, proceed.

Fine, continue.

QUINCE

Robin Starveling, the tailor.

Robin Starveling, the tailor.

STARVELING

Here, Peter Quince.

Here, Peter Quince.

QUINCE

Robin Starveling, you must play Thisby's mother.

Robyn, you must be Thisby's mother.

Tom Snout, the tinker.

Tom Snout, the repairman.

SNOUT

Here, Peter Quince.

Here, Peter Quince.

QUINCE

You, Pyramus' father: myself, Thisby's father:

You are Pyramus father, and I will play Thisby's father.

Snug, the joiner; you, the lion's part: and, I

Snug the wood worker, you will be the lion, and

hope, here is a play fitted.

I think that is everyone.

SNUG

Have you the lion's part written? pray you, if it

Is the lion's part finished? If so, please

be, give it me, for I am slow of study.

let me have it. It takes me a while to learn the lines.

QUINCE

You may do it extempore, for it is nothing but roaring.

You can make it all up, because it is simply roaring.

BOTTOM

Let me play the lion too: I will roar, that I will

Then let me play the lion as well. I will roar

do any man's heart good to hear me; I will roar,

so forcefully and everyone will love it,

that I will make the duke say 'Let him roar again,

and the duke will ask for me to roar

let him roar again.'

again and again.

QUINCE

An you should do it too terribly, you would fright

Then you would be too ferocious, and scare

the duchess and the ladies, that they would shriek;

the duchess and the women, and they would scream.

and that were enough to hang us all.

That would be enough to hang us all.

ALL

That would hang us, every mother's son.

They would hang every one of us!

BOTTOM

I grant you, friends, if that you should fright the

Granted, if I were to scare

ladies out of their wits, they would have no more

the women out of their minds, they would

discretion but to hang us: but I will aggravate my

surely hang us – but then I would change my

voice so that I will roar you as gently as any

voice so that my roar will be as gentle

sucking dove; I will roar you an 'twere any

as a dove, and when I roar you will think I was

nightingale.

a nightingale.

QUINCE

84

You can play no part but Pyramus; for Pyramus is a

You will play only Pyramus since Pyramus

sweet-faced man; a proper man, as one shall see in a

is a good lucking man, a noble man like one you would

summer's day; a most lovely gentleman-like man:

find in the summer, a handsome and chivalrous man.

therefore you must needs play Pyramus.

You are the only one who can be such a man.

BOTTOM

Well, I will undertake it. What beard were I best

Fine, I will do it. And how would you like my beard

to play it in?

to look for the part?

QUINCE

Why, what you will.

However you want.

BOTTOM

I will discharge it in either your straw-colour

I could wear a straw colored

beard, your orange-tawny beard, your purple-in-grain

beard, or an orange-red one, or a darker red

beard, or your French-crown-colour beard, your

beard, or one as yellow as the French coin called a crown.

perfect yellow.

QUINCE

Some of your French crowns have no hair at all, and

Some French kings have no hair at all,

then you will play bare-faced. But, masters, here

so you would have to go without a beard. Anyway, here

are your parts: and I am to entreat you, request

is everyone's part. I must beg and ask

you and desire you, to con them by to-morrow night;

you all to learn them by tomorrow night.

and meet me in the palace wood, a mile without the

We will meet in the forest, about a mile

town, by moonlight; there will we rehearse, for if

from town, and rehearse by the moonlight. If

we meet in the city, we shall be dogged with

we were to meet in the city, people would discover us

company, and our devices known. In the meantime I

and the play, and ruin it. In the meantime,

will draw a bill of properties, such as our play

I will list everything we need for the play.

wants. I pray you, fail me not.

Please, do everything I ask.

BOTTOM

We will meet; and there we may rehearse most

We will meet and rehearse

obscenely and courageously. Take pains; be perfect: adieu.

loudly and wonderfully. Work hard. Learn it perfectly. Goodbye.

QUINCE

At the duke's oak we meet.

In the forest by the palace we will meet.

BOTTOM

Enough; hold or cut bow-strings.

Ok, be there or do not meet us again.

Exeunt

Act II

Scene I
A wood near Athens.

Enter, from opposite sides, a FAIRY, and PUCK

PUCK

How now, spirit! whither wander you?

Hello, spirit! Where are you going?

FAIRY

Over hill, over dale,

Over hill and valley

Thorough bush, thorough brier,

and through the bush and thorns,

Over park, over pale,

over parks and gardens

Thorough flood, thorough fire,

and through the water and the fire.

I do wander everywhere,

I go everywhere

Swifter than the moon's sphere;

faster than it takes the moon to rise and fall

And I serve the fairy queen,

In order to serve the queen of the fairies

To dew her orbs upon the green.

By watering the flowers with dew.

The cowslips tall her pensioners be:

The cowslip flowers guard her –

In their gold coats spots you see;

Do you see the spots in their golden petals?

Those be rubies, fairy favours,

Those are rubies, fairy gifts,

In those freckles live their savours:

And that is where their sweet smell comes from.

I must go seek some dewdrops here

I must find some dewdrops

And hang a pearl in every cowslip's ear.

And hang one on each cowslip flower.

Farewell, thou lob of spirits; I'll be gone:

Goodbye, you bad fairy – I must leave

Our queen and all our elves come here anon.

Since the queen and the elves will be here soon.

PUCK

The king doth keep his revels here to-night:

The king is having a party here tonight

Take heed the queen come not within his sight;

So be careful to keep the queen away –

For Oberon is passing fell and wrath,

King Oberon is very angry

Because that she as her attendant hath

Since Queen Titania took a new servant,

A lovely boy, stolen from an Indian king;

A beautiful human boy stolen from an Indian king.

She never had so sweet a changeling;

She had never stolen so sweet an orphan

And jealous Oberon would have the child

And so Oberon is jealous and desires the boy

Knight of his train, to trace the forests wild;

As his servant when he wanders the wild forests.

But she perforce withholds the loved boy,

The queen refuses to give him her boy

Crowns him with flowers and makes him all her joy:

And dotes on him, putting flowers in his hair.

And now they never meet in grove or green,

Now, they never meet together in the woods

By fountain clear, or spangled starlight sheen,

Or by a clear pond, or under the night sky,

But, they do square, that all their elves for fear

Except to argue so fiercely that their elves

Creep into acorn-cups and hide them there.

Hide in acorn shells from them.

FAIRY

Either I mistake your shape and making quite,

Either I am mistaken

Or else you are that shrewd and knavish sprite

Or you are that cunning prankster fairy

Call'd Robin Goodfellow: are not you he

Named Robin Goodfellow. Isn't it you

That frights the maidens of the villagery;

Who scares the women in the village,

Skim milk, and sometimes labour in the quern

Who skims the cream off of the milk, and sometimes increase the work

And bootless make the breathless housewife churn;

Of the housewife who is trying to churn butter

And sometime make the drink to bear no barm;

By making it stay milk?

Mislead night-wanderers, laughing at their harm?

Isn't it you who makes wanderers lost and laughs at them?

Those that Hobgoblin call you and sweet Puck,

Some call you Hobgoblin or Puck,

You do their work, and they shall have good luck:

And whoever does gets your help, and you give them good luck.

Are not you he?

Isn't that you?

PUCK

Thou speak'st aright;

You are correct,

I am that merry wanderer of the night.

I am that happy traveler of the night.

I jest to Oberon and make him smile

I make jokes for King Oberon and make him smile –

When I a fat and bean-fed horse beguile,

Sometimes by tricking a calm, domestic horse

Neighing in likeness of a filly foal:

By neighing and tricking him that I am a young filly –

And sometime lurk I in a gossip's bowl,

And sometimes I hide in an old woman's bowl of ale

In very likeness of a roasted crab,

Looking like a roasted crabapple

And when she drinks, against her lips I bob

And when she drinks, I bob up to her lips

And on her wither'd dewlap pour the ale.

Making her spill the drink all over her wrinkled neck.

The wisest aunt, telling the saddest tale,

A wise aunt telling a sad story

Sometime for three-foot stool mistaketh me;

Sometimes mistakes me for a three-foot high stool

Then slip I from her bum, down topples she,

And then when she sits, I slip from her rear and she falls,

And 'tailor' cries, and falls into a cough;

Crying out in pain and coughing –

And then the whole quire hold their hips and laugh,

Then everyone laughs, holding their sides,

And waxen in their mirth and neeze and swear

And have fun, and sneeze and swear:

A merrier hour was never wasted there.

A more joyful time was never had.

But, room, fairy! here comes Oberon.

But make way, fairy! Oberon is coming.

FAIRY

And here my mistress. Would that he were gone!

And here is Queen Titania! I wish he were gone!

Enter, from one side, OBERON, with his train; from the other, TITANIA, with hers

OBERON

Ill met by moonlight, proud Titania.

It makes me feel ill to see you, Titania.

TITANIA

What, jealous Oberon! Fairies, skip hence:

Are you jealous, Oberon? Fairies, come along:

I have forsworn his bed and company.

I have promised not to sleep with him or speak to him.

OBERON

Tarry, rash wanton: am not I thy lord?

Stay, impulsive witch: aren't I your King, and husband?

TITANIA

Then I must be thy lady: but I know

Then I must be your Queen and wife, but I know

When thou hast stolen away from fairy land,

That you snuck away from fairy-land

And in the shape of Corin sat all day,

And changed your shape to that of a shepherd, spending all day

Playing on pipes of corn and versing love

Playing music and reciting love poetry

To amorous Phillida. Why art thou here,

To your fling, Phillida. And why did you come here,

Come from the farthest Steppe of India?

So far from our land in India?

But that, forsooth, the bouncing Amazon,

I know why: that swaggering Amazon

Your buskin'd mistress and your warrior love,

who was your animal skin wearing, warrior of a mistress and love,

To Theseus must be wedded, and you come

Is marrying Theseus, and you have come

To give their bed joy and prosperity.

To celebrate and bless their union.

OBERON

How canst thou thus for shame, Titania,

How can you speak so shamelessly, Titania,

Glance at my credit with Hippolyta,

And attack my thoughts of Hippolyta,

Knowing I know thy love to Theseus?

When you know that I know of your love for Theseus?

Didst thou not lead him through the glimmering night

Didn't you lead him through the night away from

From Perigenia, whom he ravished?

Perigenia, whom he raped?

And make him with fair AEgle break his faith,

And didn't you make him cheat on Aegle

With Ariadne and Antiopa?

With both Ariadne and Antiopa?

TITANIA

These are the forgeries of jealousy:

You are making this up from your jealousy.

And never, since the middle summer's spring,

Never, since the beginning of midsummer,

Met we on hill, in dale, forest or mead,

Can I meet with the fairies, not on a hill or in the valley, or the forest,

By paved fountain or by rushy brook,

Not by a fountain or by a stream

Or in the beached margent of the sea,

Or on the beach next to the sea.

To dance our ringlets to the whistling wind,

We aren't able to dance and shake our hair in the wind

But with thy brawls thou hast disturb'd our sport.

Without you interrupting us to argue and fight.

Therefore the winds, piping to us in vain,

So, the winds, making noise in vain,

As in revenge, have suck'd up from the sea

Have taken their revenge by lifting up from the sea

Contagious fogs; which falling in the land

Great clouds that rain all over the land,

Have every pelting river made so proud

Pelting the river until each one is puffed up, like they are proud,

That they have overborne their continents:

Spilling over their banks and flooding.

The ox hath therefore stretch'd his yoke in vain,

The ox in the fields can't pull the yoke through the wet mud,

The ploughman lost his sweat, and the green corn

The farmer can do nothing, and the young corn

Hath rotted ere his youth attain'd a beard;

Has rotted before it grew out its yellow tassel marking its ripeness.

The fold stands empty in the drowned field,

The sheep pens are empty in the flooded fields,

And crows are fatted with the murrion flock;

And crows are fat from eating the sheep who died from disease.

The nine men's morris is fill'd up with mud,

Places where people could play games like "nine men's morris" are now muddy,

And the quaint mazes in the wanton green

And mazes cut into fields of weeds

For lack of tread are undistinguishable:

Have collapsed from the water and are unusable.

The human mortals want their winter here;

Since it is not winter for the humans,

No night is now with hymn or carol blest:

They have not blessed the night with their songs to protect them,

Therefore the moon, the governess of floods,

And so the moon, who controls the water,

Pale in her anger, washes all the air,

Can put water into the air in her anger

That rheumatic diseases do abound:

Which causes sicknesses to arise.

And thorough this distemperature we see

And since the temperatures are off for the time of year,

The seasons alter: hoary-headed frosts

The seasons are changing: frosts

Far in the fresh lap of the crimson rose,

Are appearing on the blooming rose

And on old Hiems' thin and icy crown

And on Winter's crown of ice,

An odorous chaplet of sweet summer buds

A row of sweet smelling flowers, like prayer beads,

Is, as in mockery, set: the spring, the summer,

hangs like a joke. Spring, summer,

The childing autumn, angry winter, change

fertile autumn, and cold, angry winter, have exchanged

Their wonted liveries, and the mazed world,

their places, and now the confused world

By their increase, now knows not which is which:

doesn't know which season it is in.

And this same progeny of evils comes

This list of evils and poor effects all come

From our debate, from our dissension;

For our arguments and disagreement:

We are their parents and original.

We are the causes.

OBERON

Do you amend it then; it lies in you:

Then fix it: you are the one at fault.

Why should Titania cross her Oberon?

Why are you being mean to me?

I do but beg a little changeling boy,

All I want is a little orphan boy

To be my henchman.

To be my servant.

TITANIA

Set your heart at rest:

Let it go:

The fairy land buys not the child of me.

You cannot buy the child from me for all of fairy-land.

His mother was a votaress of my order:

His mother worshipped me as part of my order,

And, in the spiced Indian air, by night,

And at night, in the perfumed Indian air,

Full often hath she gossip'd by my side,

She gossiped with me at my side,

And sat with me on Neptune's yellow sands,

And sat with me on the yellow sands of the beach,

Marking the embarked traders on the flood,

Watching the traders in their ships out at sea,

When we have laugh'd to see the sails conceive

And laughing to watch the sails grow,

And grow big-bellied with the wanton wind;

Like a pregnant woman's belly, with the wind.

Which she, with pretty and with swimming gait

She, beautiful and graceful,

Following,--her womb then rich with my young squire,--

And already pregnant with the boy you want,

Would imitate, and sail upon the land,

Would imitate the ships and pretend to sail on the land,

To fetch me trifles, and return again,

Fetching me little gifts and returning

As from a voyage, rich with merchandise.

Like she had been on a voyage and came back with treasures.

But she, being mortal, of that boy did die;

But she was mortal, and she died giving birth to the boy

And for her sake do I rear up her boy,

Whom now I raise for her sake,

And for her sake I will not part with him.

And for her sake I will not give him to you.

OBERON

How long within this wood intend you stay?

How long are you staying in this forest?

TITANIA

Perchance till after Theseus' wedding-day.

Probably until after Theseus' wedding.

If you will patiently dance in our round

If you can dance with us nicely

And see our moonlight revels, go with us;

And partake in our parties beneath the moon, then come with us,

If not, shun me, and I will spare your haunts.

And if not, leave me alone and I will leave you alone.

OBERON

Give me that boy, and I will go with thee.

Give me the boy and I will go with you.

TITANIA

Not for thy fairy kingdom. Fairies, away!

Not for the entire kingdom. Fairies, come!

We shall chide downright, if I longer stay.

We will fight openly if I longer stay.

Exit TITANIA with her train

OBERON

Well, go thy way: thou shalt not from this grove

Fine, go your way. You won't leave here

Till I torment thee for this injury.

Until I get my revenge for this.

My gentle Puck, come hither. Thou rememberest

Puck, come here. Do you remember

Since once I sat upon a promontory,

when I sat on a cliff

And heard a mermaid on a dolphin's back

And heard a mermaid riding on a dolphin,

Uttering such dulcet and harmonious breath

Singing such a sweet melody

That the rude sea grew civil at her song

That it made the stormy sea become calm

And certain stars shot madly from their spheres,

And the stars twinkled brighter

To hear the sea-maid's music.

just to hear her song?

PUCK

I remember.

OBERON

That very time I saw, but thou couldst not,

Also then, I saw something you couldn't:

Flying between the cold moon and the earth,

Flying high in the sky, between the moon and earth,

Cupid all arm'd: a certain aim he took

Was Cupid, armed iwth his bow. He took aim

At a fair vestal throned by the west,

At a vestal virgin, a worshipper sitting on a throne in the west

And loosed his love-shaft smartly from his bow,

And shot an enchanted arrow from his bow strongly,

As it should pierce a hundred thousand hearts;

As if he was trying to shoot it through a hundred thousand hearts at once.

But I might see young Cupid's fiery shaft

But I saw this enflamed arrow of Cupid's

Quench'd in the chaste beams of the watery moon,

Put out by the virginal beams of the moon

And the imperial votaress passed on,

And so the young royal worshipper walked on

In maiden meditation, fancy-free.

Meditating beautifully, and spared from the arrow.

Yet mark'd I where the bolt of Cupid fell:

But, I saw where the arrow fell:

It fell upon a little western flower,

It struck a little wester flower

Before milk-white, now purple with love's wound,

That had been milk white, but after turned purple where the arrow hit it.

And maidens call it love-in-idleness.

Maidens refer to it as "love-in-idleness."

Fetch me that flower; the herb I shew'd thee once:

Bring me that flower, the one I once showed you.

The juice of it on sleeping eye-lids laid

If its juice is put on the eyelids of someone asleep,

Will make or man or woman madly dote

It will make any man, woman, or creature fall in love

Upon the next live creature that it sees.

With the next living creature it sees.

Fetch me this herb; and be thou here again

Bring me this flower and return

Ere the leviathan can swim a league.

Before the great sea monster can swim a league.

PUCK

I'll put a girdle round about the earth

I can circle the earth

In forty minutes.

In forty minutes.

Exit

OBERON

Having once this juice,

Once I have this flower and its potion,

I'll watch Titania when she is asleep,

I will go to Titania when she is asleep

And drop the liquor of it in her eyes.

And place a drop of it in her eyes.

The next thing then she waking looks upon,

When she wakes, the next thing she sees,

Be it on lion, bear, or wolf, or bull,

Whether it is a lion, bear, wolf, bull

On meddling monkey, or on busy ape,

A bothersome monkey, or an ape,

She shall pursue it with the soul of love:

She will fall in love with it and pursue it.

And ere I take this charm from off her sight,

Then, before I remove this potion –

As I can take it with another herb,

Since I can do that with another flower –

I'll make her render up her page to me.

I will force her to give me the orphan boy.

But who comes here? I am invisible;

Who is coming now? Since I am invisible

And I will overhear their conference.

I will overhear their conversation.

Enter DEMETRIUS, HELENA, following him

DEMETRIUS

I love thee not, therefore pursue me not.

I don't love you, now stop following me.

Where is Lysander and fair Hermia?

Where are Lysander and beautiful Hermia?

The one I'll slay, the other slayeth me.

I will kill Lysander, while Hermia has me head over heels for her.

Thou told'st me they were stolen unto this wood;

You told me they had snuck off into this forest,

And here am I, and wode within this wood,

And here I am, going crazy in a forest,

Because I cannot meet my Hermia.

All because I can't meet Hermia.

Hence, get thee gone, and follow me no more.

Now go away and stop following me.

HELENA

You draw me, you hard-hearted adamant;

You attract me like a cruel magnet,

But yet you draw not iron, for my heart

One that must not attract iron because my heart

Is true as steel: leave you your power to draw,

Is pure, like steel. Stop pulling me to you

And I shall have no power to follow you.

And I will not be forced to follow you.

DEMETRIUS

Do I entice you? do I speak you fair?

Do I flirt with you? Do I speak kindly to you?

Or, rather, do I not in plainest truth

Or instead, am I honest with you

Tell you, I do not, nor I cannot love you?

By saying that I do not and cannot love you?

HELENA

And even for that do I love you the more.

Even that makes me love you more.

I am your spaniel; and, Demetrius,

I am your pet dog, Demetrius:

The more you beat me, I will fawn on you:

Though you beat me, I still come to you.

Use me but as your spaniel, spurn me, strike me,

Use me like a dog, turn me away, hit me,

Neglect me, lose me; only give me leave,

Ignore me – just allow me,

Unworthy as I am, to follow you.

Though I am unworthy, to follow you.

What worser place can I beg in your love,--

Is there any lower place in your life –

And yet a place of high respect with me,--

And yet I would be honored to be treated this way –

Than to be used as you use your dog?

Than to be used, to be your dog?

DEMETRIUS

Tempt not too much the hatred of my spirit;

Don't tempt me to be even more hateful to you.

For I am sick when I do look on thee.

I feel sick when I look at you.

HELENA

And I am sick when I look not on you.

And I feel sick when I do not look at you.

DEMETRIUS

You do impeach your modesty too much,

You are risking your reputation of modesy

To leave the city and commit yourself

By leaving the city and trusting

Into the hands of one that loves you not;

Someone who does not love you

To trust the opportunity of night

And to leave yourself vulnerable at night

And the ill counsel of a desert place

In the secrecy of a deserted place, far from town,

With the rich worth of your virginity.

When your valuable virginity could be taken away.

HELENA

Your virtue is my privilege: for that

I know you are virtuous, and that protects me.

It is not night when I do see your face,

Anyway, your face is so bright when I look at it

Therefore I think I am not in the night;

That I do not think it is night time.

Nor doth this wood lack worlds of company,

This forest, too, is not deserted

For you in my respect are all the world:

Because having you nearby is the same as having the whole world.

Then how can it be said I am alone,

So how can you say I am alone

When all the world is here to look on me?

When the whole world is here with me?

DEMETRIUS

I'll run from thee and hide me in the brakes,

I'll run away and hide in the brush,

And leave thee to the mercy of wild beasts.

Leaving you to the wild animals.

HELENA

The wildest hath not such a heart as you.

The wildest one is not as mean as you.

Run when you will, the story shall be changed:

Run away then, the classic myth will be reversed:

Apollo flies, and Daphne holds the chase;

Apollo will fly instead, and Daphne will chase him,

The dove pursues the griffin; the mild hind

The dove will chase the griffin, the deer

Makes speed to catch the tiger; bootless speed,

Will run fast after the tiger, with unmatched speed

When cowardice pursues and valour flies.

What is cowardly will chase what is brave, which runs away.

DEMETRIUS

I will not stay thy questions; let me go:

I will not listen to your questions, let me leave –

Or, if thou follow me, do not believe

Or, if you follow me, know

But I shall do thee mischief in the wood.

That I will do evil things to you in the forest.

HELENA

Ay, in the temple, in the town, the field,

Already in the temple and in the town and in the field

108

You do me mischief. Fie, Demetrius!

You do evil things to me! Bad Demetrius!

Your wrongs do set a scandal on my sex:

Your evil treatment insults women

We cannot fight for love, as men may do;

Who cannot fight for love like men do,

We should be wood and were not made to woo.

Instead we should be the ones courted, not the courters.

Exit DEMETRIUS

I'll follow thee and make a heaven of hell,

I'll follow you and the evil you give will be heaven and joy to me,

To die upon the hand I love so well.

Even joy to be killed by someone I love so much.

Exit

OBERON

Fare thee well, nymph: ere he do leave this grove,

Good luck, young girl. Before Demetrius leaves the forest,

Thou shalt fly him and he shall seek thy love.

You will be running from him, and he will be chasing you.

Re-enter PUCK

Hast thou the flower there? Welcome, wanderer.

Do you have the flower? Hello, wandering Puck.

PUCK

Ay, there it is.

Yes, here it is.

OBERON

I pray thee, give it me.

Please, give it to me.

I know a bank where the wild thyme blows,

There is a bank I know where wild thyme

Where oxlips and the nodding violet grows,

And oxlip and violet flowers grow,

Quite over-canopied with luscious woodbine,

Shaded by overgrowths of honeysuckle

With sweet musk-roses and with eglantine:

And musk-roses and sweet briars:

There sleeps Titania sometime of the night,

Sometimes Titania sleeps there at night

Lull'd in these flowers with dances and delight;

Attracted to the flowers after her dancing and frolicking.

And there the snake throws her enamell'd skin,

There, the snake covers her in a blanket of its shed skin

Weed wide enough to wrap a fairy in:

And the fairies wrap themselves in the wide weeds,

And with the juice of this I'll streak her eyes,

It is there that I will place this potion on her eyes

110

And make her full of hateful fantasies.

And make her fall madly in love.

Take thou some of it, and seek through this grove:

Now you take some of it as well, and look for

A sweet Athenian lady is in love

A sweet Athenian lady who is in love

With a disdainful youth: anoint his eyes;

With a young man who does not love her. Put this on his eyes,

But do it when the next thing he espies

But do it so that the next thing he sees

May be the lady: thou shalt know the man

Is the woman. You will know the man

By the Athenian garments he hath on.

By his Athenian clothing.

Effect it with some care, that he may prove

Make sure you apply the potion so that he

More fond on her than she upon her love:

Will love her more than she loves him,

And look thou meet me ere the first cock crow.

And then meet me before the first crowing of the rooster.

PUCK

Fear not, my lord, your servant shall do so.

Don't worry, my king, I will do everything you ask.

Exeunt

Scene II
Another part of the wood.

Enter TITANIA, with her train

TITANIA

Come, now a roundel and a fairy song;

Come and we will dance and sing,

Then, for the third part of a minute, hence;

And then, for a little while after,

Some to kill cankers in the musk-rose buds,

Some of you will kill worms infecting the flowers

Some war with rere-mice for their leathern wings,

And some fight the bats to take their leathery wings

To make my small elves coats, and some keep back

So I can make coats from them for small elves, and some of you

The clamorous owl that nightly hoots and wonders

Will chase off that noisy owl that hoots every night

At our quaint spirits. Sing me now asleep;

At our festivities. Now, sing me to sleep,

Then to your offices and let me rest.

And then go to work and let me rest.

The Fairies sing

FIRST FAIRY

You spotted snakes with double tongue,

You forked tongue snakes

Thorny hedgehogs, be not seen;

And porcupines, go away;

Newts and blind-worms, do no wrong,

Newts and lizards, do not do anything wrong,

Come not near our fairy queen.

And stay away from Queen Titania.

FAIRIES
Philomel, with melody

Dear nightingale, melodiously

Sing in our sweet lullaby;

Sing with us in this lullaby.

Lulla, lulla, lullaby, lulla, lulla, lullaby:

Never harm,

Let no harm

Nor spell nor charm,

Or spell or enchantment

Come our lovely lady nigh;

Come to our lovely queen here.

So, good night, with lullaby.

Now goodnight, and sweet dreams.

FIRST FAIRY

Weaving spiders, come not here;

Spiders weaving your webs, stay away,

Hence, you long-legg'd spinners, hence!

All of you long-legged spinners of webs, stay back!

Beetles black, approach not near;

Black beetles, do not come near,

Worm nor snail, do no offence.

And worm and snail, do nothing wrong.

FAIRIES

Philomel, with melody

Dear nightingale, melodiously

Sing in our sweet lullaby;

Sing with us in this lullaby.

Lulla, lulla, lullaby, lulla, lulla, lullaby:

Never harm,

Let no harm

Nor spell nor charm,

Or spell or enchantment

Come our lovely lady nigh;

Come to our lovely queen here.

So, good night, with lullaby.

Now goodnight, and sweet dreams.

FAIRY

Hence, away! now all is well:

Stop, and let us go! Everything is well.

One aloof stand sentinel.

One of you stay here to guard.

Exeunt Fairies. TITANIA sleeps

Enter OBERON and squeezes the flower on TITANIA's eyelids

OBERON

What thou seest when thou dost wake,

Whatever you see when you wake up

Do it for thy true-love take,

You will believe is your true love.

Love and languish for his sake:

Love, and feel the pain of love for the sake of the orphan boy,

Be it ounce, or cat, or bear,

Whether it is a snow leopard, or a cat, or a bear

Pard, or boar with bristled hair,

Or a leopard, or a bristled boar –

In thy eye that shall appear

In your eye it will appear,

When thou wakest, it is thy dear:

When you wake, as your beloved:

Wake when some vile thing is near.

So I hope you wake when something nasty is near.

Exit

Enter LYSANDER and HERMIA

LYSANDER

Fair love, you faint with wandering in the wood;

My love, you look weak from walking so much in this forest,

And to speak troth, I have forgot our way:

And to tell the truth, I have gotten lost.

We'll rest us, Hermia, if you think it good,

We should rest now, Hermia, if you think that's a good idea,

And tarry for the comfort of the day.

And wait for daylight.

HERMIA

Be it so, Lysander: find you out a bed;

I agree with you, Lysander: find yourself a bed,

For I upon this bank will rest my head.

because I will rest against this bank.

LYSANDER

One turf shall serve as pillow for us both;

It will be a pillow for both of us,

One heart, one bed, two bosoms and one troth.

One pillow, for one bed, for one heart shared by two people with one truth.

HERMIA

Nay, good Lysander; for my sake, my dear,

No, good Lysander, please, my love,

Lie further off yet, do not lie so near.

Find a place farther away, do not sleep so close to me.

LYSANDER

O, take the sense, sweet, of my innocence!

Oh my dear, please recognize my good intentions!

Love takes the meaning in love's conference.

Those in love should understand each other.

I mean, that my heart unto yours is knit

What I mean is that my heart is tied to yours

So that but one heart we can make of it;

So that we have, in essence, one heart:

Two bosoms interchained with an oath;

Two people bound with a single oath,

So then two bosoms and a single troth.

Two people who share one truth.

Then by your side no bed-room me deny;

So do not deny me space to sleep beside you–

For lying so, Hermia, I do not lie.

By lying there, I will not lie to your honor and disrespect you.

HERMIA

Lysander riddles very prettily:

Lysander speaks very nicely:

Now much beshrew my manners and my pride,

I would betray my manners and honor

If Hermia meant to say Lysander lied.

If I were to imply that Lysander was a liar.

But, gentle friend, for love and courtesy

But, my friend, for love and politeness,

Lie further off; in human modesty,

Lie farther away. It is modest

Such separation as may well be said

For such separation to be between

Becomes a virtuous bachelor and a maid,

A virtuous bachelor and a virtuous maid,

So far be distant; and, good night, sweet friend:

So be distant. And now, goodnight sweet friend:

Thy love ne'er alter till thy sweet life end!

I hope your love never changes until your dear life ends!

LYSANDER

Amen, amen, to that fair prayer, say I;

I say amen to that prayer,

And then end life when I end loyalty!

And I hope my life ends if I should be disloyal to you!

Here is my bed: sleep give thee all his rest!

I will sleep over here, sleep well and be rested!

HERMIA

With half that wish the wisher's eyes be press'd!

You too, Lysander, sleep well also!

They sleep.

Enter PUCK

PUCK

Through the forest have I gone.

I have gone through the entire forest

But Athenian found I none,

But have not found the Athenian

On whose eyes I might approve

Whose eyes I must drug

This flower's force in stirring love.

With this flower's potion to enchant him.

Night and silence.--Who is here?

Only night and silence – but who is this?

Weeds of Athens he doth wear:

He wears Athenian clothing:

This is he, my master said,

It must be him, the one my master told me about,

Despised the Athenian maid;

Who turned away the Athenian girl.

And here the maiden, sleeping sound,

And here is the girl, sound asleep

On the dank and dirty ground.

On the wet and dirty ground.

Pretty soul! she durst not lie

Pretty girl! She should not lie

Near this lack-love, this kill-courtesy.

Near this cold and rude man.

Churl, upon thy eyes I throw

Scoundrel, I put on your eyes

All the power this charm doth owe.

The full force of this potion.

When thou wakest, let love forbid

I hope, when you wake up, that love keeps

Sleep his seat on thy eyelid:

Your eyes open.

So awake when I am gone;

Now wake after I leave–

For I must now to Oberon.

I must return to King Oberon.

Exit

Enter DEMETRIUS and HELENA, running

HELENA

Stay, though thou kill me, sweet Demetrius.

Wait, Demetrius, even if you kill me!

DEMETRIUS

I charge thee, hence, and do not haunt me thus.

I beg you, leave and do not keep following me.

HELENA

O, wilt thou darkling leave me? do not so.

Oh please do not leave me alone in the dark!

DEMETRIUS

Stay, on thy peril: I alone will go.

Stay at your own risk then – I can continue alone.

Exit

HELENA

O, I am out of breath in this fond chase!

I am out of breath from chasing after Demetrius!

The more my prayer, the lesser is my grace.

The more I pray for him, the less I receive in return.

Happy is Hermia, wheresoe'er she lies;

Hermia is blessed, wherever she is,

For she hath blessed and attractive eyes.

For she has beautiful eyes.

How came her eyes so bright? Not with salt tears:

How did her eyes become this beautiful? Not from the salt of tears:

If so, my eyes are oftener wash'd than hers.

If so, my eyes are washed from tears more often and would be prettier.

No, no, I am as ugly as a bear;

No, instead I am as ugly as a bear,

For beasts that meet me run away for fear:

Even animals that see me run away, scared.

Therefore no marvel though Demetrius

Therefore it's no surprise that Demetrius

Do, as a monster fly my presence thus.

Flees, as even a monster would run away from my looks.

What wicked and dissembling glass of mine

What evil and deceiving mirror

Made me compare with Hermia's sphery eyne?

Made me think I could compare to Hermia's beauty?

But who is here? Lysander! on the ground!

Who is this? Lysander! On the ground!

Dead? or asleep? I see no blood, no wound.

Is he dead or asleep? I don't see a wound or any blood.

Lysander if you live, good sir, awake.

Lysander, if you are alive, wake up!

LYSANDER

[Awaking] And run through fire I will for thy sweet sake.

And I will then run through fire for you.

Transparent Helena! Nature shows art,

Beautiful Helena! Nature has skillfully

That through thy bosom makes me see thy heart.

Made me able to see through your chest and right into your heart.

Where is Demetrius? O, how fit a word

Where is Demetrius? Oh the one who belongs

Is that vile name to perish on my sword!

To that name will die on my sword!

HELENA

Do not say so, Lysander; say not so

Don't say that, Lysander. Who

What though he love your Hermia? Lord, what though?

122

Cares if he loves Hermia? Who cares?

Yet Hermia still loves you: then be content.

Hermia loves you instead, so be at peace.

LYSANDER

Content with Hermia! No; I do repent

At peace with Hermia! No, I regret

The tedious minutes I with her have spent.

Spending these painful minutes with her.

Not Hermia but Helena I love:

I love Helena, not Hermia:

Who will not change a raven for a dove?

Who would not trade a raven for a pure dove?

The will of man is by his reason sway'd;

A man's reason guides his will

And reason says you are the worthier maid.

And my reason says you are much worthier than Hermia.

Things growing are not ripe until their season

Plants do not get ripe until they are old enough,

So I, being young, till now ripe not to reason;

And the same is true for me: I was not ripe enough to see you until now.

And touching now the point of human skill,

Now, as to human abilities:

Reason becomes the marshal to my will

Reason has changed my desires

And leads me to your eyes, where I o'erlook

And lead them to your eyes, in which I see

Love's stories written in love's richest book.

The greatest stories of love in love's best book.

HELENA

Wherefore was I to this keen mockery born?

Why was I born to be made fun of?

When at your hands did I deserve this scorn?

When have I deserved to be treated so rudely by you?

Is't not enough, is't not enough, young man,

Isn't it more than enough, young man,

That I did never, no, nor never can,

That I have never, and will never,

Deserve a sweet look from Demetrius' eye,

Receive a kind look from Demetrius?

But you must flout my insufficiency?

And on top of that now you mock my shortcomings to Hermia?

Good troth, you do me wrong, good sooth, you do,

Seriously, you are treating me evilly

In such disdainful manner me to woo.

By speaking to me so disdainfully.

But fare you well: perforce I must confess

Now, goodbye. Though first I must say

I thought you lord of more true gentleness.

That I thought you were much more noble.

O, that a lady, of one man refused.

I am already a lady one man refuses,

Should of another therefore be abused!

And now must I be one that another treats poorly?

Exit

LYSANDER

She sees not Hermia. Hermia, sleep thou there:

She didn't see Hermia. Hermia, stay asleep

And never mayst thou come Lysander near!

And never come near me again!

For as a surfeit of the sweetest things

I feel overstuffed with sweet things, like how eating desserts

The deepest loathing to the stomach brings,

Makes the stomach feel ill.

Or as tie heresies that men do leave

Or, false beliefs that men stop believing

Are hated most of those they did deceive,

Are hated most by the men they formerly deceived.

So thou, my surfeit and my heresy,

So you, Hermia, whom I have been overstuffed with, and whom I falsely believed in,

Of all be hated, but the most of me!

You will be hated most by me!

And, all my powers, address your love and might

I will turn all of my power and strength and love

To honour Helen and to be her knight!

Toward Helen in order to win her!

Exit

HERMIA

[Awaking] Help me, Lysander, help me! do thy best

Lysander, help me! Do something

To pluck this crawling serpent from my breast!

And get this snake off of me!

Ay me, for pity! what a dream was here!

Oh my! What a dream that was!

Lysander, look how I do quake with fear:

Lysander, look how much I am shivering from fright:

Methought a serpent eat my heart away,

I thought a serpent was eating my heart

And you sat smiling at his cruel pray.

While you sat by smiling and watching.

Lysander! what, removed? Lysander! lord!

Lysander! What, is he gone? Lysander!

What, out of hearing? gone? no sound, no word?

Can he not hear me? Is he gone without giving me notice?

Alack, where are you speak, an if you hear;

If you hear me speak,

Speak, of all loves! I swoon almost with fear.

Speak, Lysander! I am almost fainting from fear.

No? then I well perceive you all not nigh

No? Then I suppose you are not nearby.

Either death or you I'll find immediately.

I will either die, or find you right away.

Exit

Act III

Scene I
The wood. TITANIA lying asleep.

Enter QUINCE, SNUG, BOTTOM, FLUTE, SNOUT, and STARVELING

BOTTOM

Are we all met?

Is everyone here?

QUINCE

Pat, pat; and here's a marvellous convenient place

Everyone is on time even. This is a perfect place

for our rehearsal. This green plot shall be our

to rehearse the play. The green area over there will be

stage, this hawthorn-brake our tiring-house; and we

the stage and this large bush our dressing room. We

will do it in action as we will do it before the duke.

will perform it exactly as we will in front of the duke.

BOTTOM

Peter Quince,--

Peter Quince--

QUINCE

What sayest thou, bully Bottom?

What is it, good Bottom?

128

BOTTOM

There are things in this comedy of Pyramus and

I am worried that some parts of this comedy of Pyramus and

Thisby that will never please. First, Pyramus must

Thisby will not be acceptable. For example, Pyramus

draw a sword to kill himself; which the ladies

kills himself with a sword, something ladies

cannot abide. How answer you that?

cannot watch. What can we do about that?

SNOUT

By'r lakin, a parlous fear.

By God, that's a scary problem.

STARVELING

I believe we must leave the killing out, when all is done.

It seems we must leave out the suicide.

BOTTOM

Not a whit: I have a device to make all well.

No, we won't: I have an idea to make it work well.

Write me a prologue; and let the prologue seem to

Write a prologue that I can say before the play starts, saying

say, we will do no harm with our swords, and that

that we will not hurt anyone with our swords, and that

Pyramus is not killed indeed; and, for the more

Pyramus does not actually die – actually, even

better assurance, tell them that I, Pyramus, am not

better, tell them that I am not really

Pyramus, but Bottom the weaver: this will put them

Pyramus, but am Bottom the weaver. Saying this will

out of fear.

calm their fears.

QUINCE

Well, we will have such a prologue; and it shall be

Okay, and we will write that prologue in

written in eight and six.

ballad form.

BOTTOM

No, make it two more; let it be written in eight and eight.

No, make each line even syllables.

SNOUT

Will not the ladies be afeard of the lion?

Won't the ladies be afraid of the lion?

STARVELING

I fear it, I promise you.

I am worried about that, really.

BOTTOM

130

Masters, you ought to consider with yourselves: to

Yes, friends, we should all think about this: to

bring in--God shield us!--a lion among ladies, is a

bring a lion – a lion! – into the company of women, is an

most dreadful thing; for there is not a more fearful

awful thing. There is not a scarier

wild-fowl than your lion living; and we ought to

bird alive than a lion, and we would do well

look to 't.

to think about this.

SNOUT

Therefore another prologue must tell he is not a lion.

So why not write another prologue explaining that he is not a real lion?

BOTTOM

Nay, you must name his name, and half his face must

That's not enough: we must name the actor, and show half the face

be seen through the lion's neck: and he himself

through the lion's neck. And he should

must speak through, saying thus, or to the same

speak directly to the audience, saying something

defect,--'Ladies,'--or 'Fair-ladies--I would wish

like, "Ladies," or "Fair ladies, I hope"

You,'--or 'I would request you,'--or 'I would

or, "I would like to ask you," or "I

entreat you,--not to fear, not to tremble: my life

beg of you, do not be afraid. I am as concerned for your life

for yours. If you think I come hither as a lion, it

as I am mine. If you think I am actually a lion,

were pity of my life: no I am no such thing; I am a

I would be ashamed: I am not, I am only

man as other men are;' and there indeed let him name

a man like these other men." And then make him

his name, and tell them plainly he is Snug the joiner.

say plainly that he is Snug the joiner.

QUINCE

Well it shall be so. But there is two hard things;

Alright, that is all fine. Now there are two difficulties.

that is, to bring the moonlight into a chamber; for,

One is how to get the moonlight into the room, since

you know, Pyramus and Thisby meet by moonlight.

as you all know, Pyramus and Thisby meet beneath the moon.

SNOUT

Doth the moon shine that night we play our play?

Is there a full moon or a bright moon the night we are to perform?

BOTTOM

A calendar, a calendar! look in the almanac; find

Someone get a calendar or an almanac and find out

out moonshine, find out moonshine.

how the moon is shining that night.

QUINCE

Yes, it doth shine that night.

Yes, it is bright that night.

BOTTOM

Why, then may you leave a casement of the great

Well then all we have to do is leave open

chamber window, where we play, open, and the moon

the big window in the room where we play, and the moon

may shine in at the casement.

will shine into the room.

QUINCE

Ay; or else one must come in with a bush of thorns

Yes, that or someone could come in with a thornbush

and a lanthorn, and say he comes to disfigure, or to

and a lantern and explain that he is the representation

present, the person of Moonshine. Then, there is

of the character of Moonshine. Also, there is

another thing: we must have a wall in the great

another difficulty: we need a wall to put in the

chamber; for Pyramus and Thisby says the story, did

chamber room, since Pyramus and Thisby in the story

talk through the chink of a wall.

talk to each other through a hole in the wall.

SNOUT

You can never bring in a wall. What say you, Bottom?

We cannot bring in a wall. What do you think, Bottom?

BOTTOM

Some man or other must present Wall: and let him

Someone needs to play the Wall, then – we can give him

have some plaster, or some loam, or some rough-cast

some plaster or some clay or some gravel to put

about him, to signify wall; and let him hold his

on him so he looks like a wall, and he can hold

fingers thus, and through that cranny shall Pyramus

his fingers like this, and through that hole Pyramus

and Thisby whisper.

and Thisby can whisper.

QUINCE

If that may be, then all is well. Come, sit down,

If we can do that, then we are in good shape. Come and sit,

every mother's son, and rehearse your parts.

everyone, and rehearse your parts.

Pyramus, you begin: when you have spoken your

Pyramus, you first: after you have finished your

speech, enter into that brake: and so every one

speech go behind the bush, and everyone else, do the same thing

according to his cue.

when it is your cue to exit the stage.

134

Enter PUCK behind

PUCK

What hempen home-spuns have we swaggering here,

Who are these poorly clothed hicks prancing about

So near the cradle of the fairy queen?

So close to where the queen sleep?

What, a play toward! I'll be an auditor;

Oh so this is a play! I will be an audience member then,

An actor too, perhaps, if I see cause.

And perhaps an actor too, if I want.

QUINCE

Speak, Pyramus. Thisby, stand forth.

Speak now, Pyramus; Thisby, be ready.

BOTTOM

Thisby, the flowers of odious savours sweet,--

Thisby, these flowers of sweet, odious tastes--

QUINCE

Odours, odours.

Odors, not odious.

BOTTOM

--odours savours sweet:

--odors tastes sweet:

So hath thy breath, my dearest Thisby dear.

So does your breath, my dear Thisby.

But hark, a voice! stay thou but here awhile,

But listen, a voice! Wait here for a little

And by and by I will to thee appear.

And soon enough I will come back.

Exit

PUCK

A stranger Pyramus than e'er played here.

I have never seen a stranger Pyramus.

Exit

FLUTE

Must I speak now?

Do I go now?

QUINCE

Ay, marry, must you; for you must understand he goes

Yes, of course, now you speak. Know that at this point, he leaves

but to see a noise that he heard, and is to come again.

to check on a noise that he heard, and will then come back.

FLUTE

Most radiant Pyramus, most lily-white of hue,

Most beautiful Pyramus, as white as a lily,

Of colour like the red rose on triumphant brier,

As red as the rose on the rosebush,

Most brisky juvenal and eke most lovely Jew,

An energetic young man and a handsome Jew,

As true as truest horse that yet would never tire,

As dependable as the best horse that never gets tired,

I'll meet thee, Pyramus, at Ninny's tomb.

I'll meet you, Pyramus, at Ninny's tomb.

QUINCE

'Ninus' tomb,' man: why, you must not speak that

That's "Ninus' tomb," Flute, and you aren't supposed to say that

yet; that you answer to Pyramus: you speak all your

yet. That's your response to Pyramus: first you say

part at once, cues and all Pyramus enter: your cue

your part, and after Pyramus enters again, your cue

is past; it is, 'never tire.'

passes at "never tire," that is your last line before Pyramus speaks again.

FLUTE

O,--As true as truest horse, that yet would

I see -- As dependable as the best horse that

never tire.

never gets tired,

Re-enter PUCK, and BOTTOM with an ass's head

BOTTOM

If I were fair, Thisby, I were only thine.

If I were the most handsome man, Thisbuy, you would still be my one and only.

QUINCE

O monstrous! O strange! we are haunted. Pray,

How awful! How strange! We are being haunted! Everyone,

masters! fly, masters! Help!

pray and run away! Help!

Exeunt QUINCE, SNUG, FLUTE, SNOUT, and STARVELING

PUCK

I'll follow you, I'll lead you about a round,

I'll follow you and lead you in a circle,

Through bog, through bush, through brake, through brier:

Through bogs and bushes, through thickets and thorns:

Sometime a horse I'll be, sometime a hound,

Sometimes I'll be a horse, and sometimes a dog,

A hog, a headless bear, sometime a fire;

Sometimes a pig, or a headless bear, or a fire,

And neigh, and bark, and grunt, and roar, and burn,

And I will neigh, bark, grunt, roar and burn,

Like horse, hound, hog, bear, fire, at every turn.

Like each of those things to scare you common-folk.

Exit

BOTTOM

Why do they run away? this is a knavery of them to

Why are they running away? This is some mean joke

make me afeard.

they are doing to scare me.

Re-enter SNOUT

SNOUT

O Bottom, thou art changed! what do I see on thee?

Bottom, you have been turned into something else! What is this on your neck?

BOTTOM

What do you see? you see an asshead of your own, do

What are you talking about? You are acting like an ass.

you?

Exit SNOUT

Re-enter QUINCE

QUINCE

Bless thee, Bottom! bless thee! thou art

God bless you, Bottom! You have been

translated.

changed into something else!

Exit

BOTTOM

I see their knavery: this is to make an ass of me;

I see right through their joke. They are trying to make me a fool

to fright me, if they could. But I will not stir

and frighten me, but I will not leave

from this place, do what they can: I will walk up

here, no matter what they do to me. I will walk all

and down here, and I will sing, that they shall hear

around, and I will sing, and they will hear me and know

I am not afraid.

that I am not afraid.

Sings

The ousel cock so black of hue,

The blackbird, feathers so black,

With orange-tawny bill,

With a dark brown bill,

The throstle with his note so true,

The thrush with his pure song

The wren with little quill,--

And the wren with its small feathers--

140

TITANIA

[Awaking] What angel wakes me from my flowery bed?

Who is this waking me from my bed of flowers with the voice of an angel?

BOTTOM

[Sings]

The finch, the sparrow and the lark,

The finch, the sparrow, and the lark,

The plain-song cuckoo gray,

The gray cuckoo who sings a plain song,

Whose note full many a man doth mark,

Whose words many men hear

And dares not answer nay;--

And do not dare to say no to --

for, indeed, who would set his wit to so foolish

Because really, who would be rash enough to set himself agains such a silly

a bird? who would give a bird the lie, though he cry

bird? Who would so completely doubt the bird and think his cry

'cuckoo' never so?

that points out the cuckold is wrong?

TITANIA

I pray thee, gentle mortal, sing again:

Please, mortal human, sing again;

Mine ear is much enamour'd of thy note;

I love to hear your beautiful voice,

So is mine eye enthralled to thy shape;

And I love to look on your handsome shape.

And thy fair virtue's force perforce doth move me

All of your good qualities move me

On the first view to say, to swear, I love thee.

On first sight and they make me swear that I love you.

BOTTOM

Methinks, mistress, you should have little reason

Lady, I think you have very little reason

for that: and yet, to say the truth, reason and

for that. But on the other hand, truth, reason, and

love keep little company together now-a-days; the

love do not often go together...

more the pity that some honest neighbours will not

it's too bad some mutual neighbors do not

make them friends. Nay, I can gleek upon occasion.

introduce them to each other. Oh but I am only joking.

TITANIA

Thou art as wise as thou art beautiful.

You are as wise as you are beautiful.

BOTTOM

Not so, neither: but if I had wit enough to get out

I am not that either. But if I had enough brains to get out

of this wood, I have enough to serve mine own turn.

of this forest, I would have enough for my life.

142

TITANIA

Out of this wood do not desire to go:

Do not wish to leave this forest:

Thou shalt remain here, whether thou wilt or no.

You will stay here, whether you want to or not.

I am a spirit of no common rate;

I am not some common spirit –

The summer still doth tend upon my state;

Even the summer does what I want it to –

And I do love thee: therefore, go with me;

And I love you, so you will come with me.

I'll give thee fairies to attend on thee,

I will give you fairies to be your servants

And they shall fetch thee jewels from the deep,

And they will get you jewels from the ocean

And sing while thou on pressed flowers dost sleep;

And sing while you sleep on the flowers.

And I will purge thy mortal grossness so

I will purge your mortal humanness

That thou shalt like an airy spirit go.

Until you are a spirit like me.

Peaseblossom! Cobweb! Moth! and Mustardseed!

Peaseblossom, Cobweb, Moth, and Mustardseed!

Enter PEASEBLOSSOM, COBWEB, MOTH, and MUSTARDSEED

PEASEBLOSSOM

Ready.

I'm ready.

COBWEB

And I.

Me too.

MOTH

And I.

Me too.

MUSTARDSEED

And I.

And me.

ALL

Where shall we go?

Where should we go?

TITANIA

Be kind and courteous to this gentleman;

Treat this man kindly and politely.

Hop in his walks and gambol in his eyes;

Jump and dance in front of him,

Feed him with apricocks and dewberries,

Feed him apricots and blackberries,

With purple grapes, green figs, and mulberries;

And grapes, figs, and mulberries.

The honey-bags steal from the humble-bees,

Steal honey from the bumblebees for him

And for night-tapers crop their waxen thighs

And make candles from their wax

And light them at the fiery glow-worm's eyes,

Which you can light with the glowworm's eyes,

To have my love to bed and to arise;

So my love will have light when he goes to bed and wakes up.

And pluck the wings from Painted butterflies

Pluck the wings of butterflies

To fan the moonbeams from his sleeping eyes:

And use them to keep the bright moonbeams from his eyes when he is asleep.

Nod to him, elves, and do him courtesies.

Bow to him, my fairy elves, and do what he wishes.

PEASEBLOSSOM

Hail, mortal!

Hello, human!

COBWEB

Hail!

Hello!

MOTH

Hail!

Hello!

MUSTARDSEED

Hail!

Hello!

BOTTOM

I cry your worships' mercy, heartily: I beseech your

Please, you fairies, tell me, what

worship's name.

are your names?

COBWEB

Cobweb.

Cobweb.

BOTTOM

I shall desire you of more acquaintance, good Master

I hope to get to know you better, Master

Cobweb: if I cut my finger, I shall make bold with

Cobweb. If I cut my finger, I can use you to bandage the wound.

you. Your name, honest gentleman?

And what is your name?

PEASEBLOSSOM

Peaseblossom.

Peaseblossom.

BOTTOM

I pray you, commend me to Mistress Squash, your

Do give my regards to your mother Mistress Squash

mother, and to Master Peascod, your father. Good

and your father, Master Peascod. I hope

Master Peaseblossom, I shall desire you of more

to know you better as well Master Peaseblossom.

acquaintance too. Your name, I beseech you, sir?

And your name?

MUSTARDSEED

Mustardseed.

Mustardseed.

BOTTOM

Good Master Mustardseed, I know your patience well:

Master Mustardseed, I know how patient you are:

that same cowardly, giant-like ox-beef hath

cuts of cow and ox have ended many

devoured many a gentleman of your house: I promise

of your relatives' lives because of their use as a condiment on the meat. And to me,

you your kindred had made my eyes water ere now. I

your relatives have made my eyes water from their pungent scent. I

desire your more acquaintance, good Master

hope to know you better, good Master

Mustardseed.

Mustardseed.

TITANIA

Come, wait upon him; lead him to my bower.

Come and wait on him, and lead him to my room.

The moon methinks looks with a watery eye;

I think the moon looks like it does when the sky is about to rain:

And when she weeps, weeps every little flower,

And when the moon rains, every little flower does as well,

Lamenting some enforced chastity.

Both grieving from being forced to abstain from sex.

Tie up my love's tongue bring him silently.

Keep my love quiet, and bring him quietly.

Exeunt

Scene II
Another part of the wood.

Enter OBERON

OBERON

I wonder if Titania be awaked;

I wonder if Titania has awoken yet.

Then, what it was that next came in her eye,

And then I wonder what came into her vision,

Which she must dote on in extremity.

What it is she is forced to love so extremely.

Enter PUCK

Here comes my messenger.

Here comes my messanger.

How now, mad spirit!

How are things, crazy spirit?

What night-rule now about this haunted grove?

What trouble have you created in this haunted forest?

PUCK

My mistress with a monster is in love.

Queen Titania is in love with a monster.

Near to her close and consecrated bower,

Near to where she sleeps,

While she was in her dull and sleeping hour,

And while she was still fast asleep,

A crew of patches, rude mechanicals,

A collective of commoners

That work for bread upon Athenian stalls,

That work for each day's bread in Athens,

Were met together to rehearse a play

Met together to rehearse a play

Intended for great Theseus' nuptial-day.

They intend to perform for Theseus' wedding.

The shallowest thick-skin of that barren sort,

The dumbest of that ugly group,

Who Pyramus presented, in their sport

Who play Pyramus,

Forsook his scene and enter'd in a brake

Left after his scene and went behind some bushes

When I did him at this advantage take,

Which is where I took advantage of him

An ass's nole I fixed on his head:

By changing his head into that of a donkey.

Anon his Thisbe must be answered,

Soon enough, Thisby called him out

And forth my mimic comes. When they him spy,

And he came forth, donkey head and all. When the group saw him,

As wild geese that the creeping fowler eye,

Like wild geese that see the hunter,

Or russet-pated choughs, many in sort,

150

Or spotted crows in a group,

Rising and cawing at the gun's report,

Rising from the ground and cawing at the sound of a gun,

Sever themselves and madly sweep the sky,

Break from the group and fly quickly away,

So, at his sight, away his fellows fly;

So to, at sight of him, his friends ran away.

And, at our stamp, here o'er and o'er one falls;

And of course here one falls again and again,

He murder cries and help from Athens calls.

While another cries out "Murder!" and seeks help from Athens.

Their sense thus weak, lost with their fears thus strong,

With their senses now weakened from their strong fear,

Made senseless things begin to do them wrong;

They made whatever was around them hurt them:

For briers and thorns at their apparel snatch;

Thorns and briars caught at their clothes,

Some sleeves, some hats, from yielders all things catch.

And sleeves and hats.

I led them on in this distracted fear,

I led them away, scared like this,

And left sweet Pyramus translated there:

And left Pyramus standing there, his head a donkey's,

When in that moment, so it came to pass,

When right at that moment, incredibly,

Titania waked and straightway loved an ass.

Titania woke up and began to love this donkey-man.

OBERON

This falls out better than I could devise.

This is better than I could have planned myself.

But hast thou yet latch'd the Athenian's eyes

And did you put the potion on the Athenian's eyes

With the love-juice, as I did bid thee do?

Like I asked you to?

PUCK

I took him sleeping,--that is finish'd too,--

I found him already asleep and finished that as well,

And the Athenian woman by his side:

The Athenian woman sleeping next to him.

That, when he waked, of force she must be eyed.

So when he wakes, she will be the one he sees.

Enter HERMIA and DEMETRIUS

OBERON

Stand close: this is the same Athenian.

Stay here, this is the same Athenian I saw earlier.

PUCK

This is the woman, but not this the man.

This is the same woman... but this is not the man I saw.

DEMETRIUS

O, why rebuke you him that loves you so?

Oh why do you scold the man who loves you so much?

Lay breath so bitter on your bitter foe.

Save your cruel words for a cruel enemy.

HERMIA

Now I but chide; but I should use thee worse,

This is nothing, but I should be treating you worse

For thou, I fear, hast given me cause to curse,

Because I'm afraid you have given me reason to curse you.

If thou hast slain Lysander in his sleep,

If you have killed Lysander while he was asleep,

Being o'er shoes in blood, plunge in the deep,

Then, since you are already walking in blood, continue on

And kill me too.

And kill me too.

The sun was not so true unto the day

The sun didn't shine on the day as steadily

As he to me: would he have stolen away

As he loved me: why would he have left

From sleeping Hermia? I'll believe as soon

Me while sleeping? I will believe that he did that as soon

This whole earth may be bored and that the moon

As the earth gets a hole drilled through it and the moon

May through the centre creep and so displease

Passes through the hole, disturbing

Her brother's noontide with Antipodes.

The tides at noon with its pull from a place opposite where it usually is.

It cannot be but thou hast murder'd him;

The only answer is that you murdered him;

So should a murderer look, so dead, so grim.

You look like a murderer anyway, so pale and ugly.

DEMETRIUS

So should the murder'd look, and so should I,

A murdered person looks like that too, which is who I really am,

Pierced through the heart with your stern cruelty:

Since you pierced my heart with your meanness.

Yet you, the murderer, look as bright, as clear,

And all the while you, the true murderer, look as beautiful

As yonder Venus in her glimmering sphere.

As the planet Venus there in the sky, glimmering.

HERMIA

What's this to my Lysander? where is he?

Why should I care about this as much as I care about Lysander? Where is he?

Ah, good Demetrius, wilt thou give him me?

Good Demetrius, please, will you give him to me?

DEMETRIUS

I had rather give his carcass to my hounds.

I'd rather give his dead body to my dogs.

HERMIA

Out, dog! out, cur! thou drivest me past the bounds

Get away from me you dog! You push me past the limits

Of maiden's patience. Hast thou slain him, then?

Of any woman's patience. Have you killed him?

Henceforth be never number'd among men!

From now on I will never consider you a man!

O, once tell true, tell true, even for my sake!

For once, tell me the truth, for my sake!

Durst thou have look'd upon him being awake,

Would you dare to even look at him while he was awake,

And hast thou kill'd him sleeping? O brave touch!

And then you killed him when he fell asleep? O, you are so brave!

Could not a worm, an adder, do so much?

Even a worm or a snake could do that.

An adder did it; for with doubler tongue

And actually a snake did do it: for you have a more forked tongue

Than thine, thou serpent, never adder stung.

Than any snake, and are more a snake than an actual snake.

DEMETRIUS

You spend your passion on a misprised mood:

You are getting too passionate on something you have misunderstood:

I am not guilty of Lysander's blood;

I am not guilty of killing Lysander –

Nor is he dead, for aught that I can tell.

In fact, for all I know he isn't even dead.

HERMIA

I pray thee, tell me then that he is well.

Please then, tell me he is alright.

DEMETRIUS

An if I could, what should I get therefore?

And if I could, what would that get me?

HERMIA

A privilege never to see me more.

The privilege of never seeing me again.

And from thy hated presence part I so:

I am leaving your presence which I hate so much:

See me no more, whether he be dead or no.

Do not see me again, whether he is dead or not.

Exit

DEMETRIUS

There is no following her in this fierce vein:

I should not follow her while she is this angry,

Here therefore for a while I will remain.

So I will stay here for a little.

So sorrow's heaviness doth heavier grow

The weight of sorrow grows even heavier

For debt that bankrupt sleep doth sorrow owe:

When one is behind on sleep.

Which now in some slight measure it will pay,

Now I'll get a little bit of that sleep back,

If for his tender here I make some stay.

And sleep here to stave off the heaviness of sorrow.

Lies down and sleeps

OBERON

What hast thou done? thou hast mistaken quite

What have you done, Puck? You have mistakenly

And laid the love-juice on some true-love's sight:

Put the love potion on someone who has true love.

Of thy misprision must perforce ensue

Of your mistakes now what has happened

Some true love turn'd and not a false turn'd true.

Is the changing of some true love, and not a false love made true.

PUCK

Then fate o'er-rules, that, one man holding troth,

Then it must be fate that made it so one man who is truly in love

A million fail, confounding oath on oath.

fails his oaths like the millions of others who naturally break these oaths.

OBERON

About the wood go swifter than the wind,

Go faster than the wind through the forest

And Helena of Athens look thou find:

And find Helena of Athens.

All fancy-sick she is and pale of cheer,

She will look sick from unrequited love, pale, and joyless,

With sighs of love, that costs the fresh blood dear:

Sighing from her pain, which makes her pale.

By some illusion see thou bring her here:

Trick her into coming here

I'll charm his eyes against she do appear.

And I will enchant him with the potion for when she gets here.

PUCK

I go, I go; look how I go,

I go, I go, look how quickly I go,

Swifter than arrow from the Tartar's bow.

Faster than an arrow shot by a Tartar.

Exit

OBERON

Flower of this purple dye,

Purple flower,

Hit with Cupid's archery,

Hit by an arrow of Cupid,

Sink in apple of his eye.

Sink into his eyes.

When his love he doth espy,

When he sees his love,

Let her shine as gloriously

Let her be as beautiful

As the Venus of the sky.

As the planet Venus up in the sky.

When thou wakest, if she be by,

When you wake, if she is nearby,

Beg of her for remedy.

Beg her to love you and cure the coming lovesickness.

Re-enter PUCK

PUCK

Captain of our fairy band,

Captain of the fairies,

Helena is here at hand;

Helena is right here

And the youth, mistook by me,

And the boy I mistook is here as well

Pleading for a lover's fee.

Pleading for her love.

Shall we their fond pageant see?

Shall we watch what they do?

Lord, what fools these mortals be!

Oh these humans are so foolish!

OBERON

Stand aside: the noise they make

Stand here, the noise they make

Will cause Demetrius to awake.

Will wake up Demetrius.

PUCK

Then will two at once woo one;

Then two of them at once will be after one:

That must needs be sport alone;

That is sport enough to watch.

And those things do best please me

These mishaps please me

That befal preposterously.

From how preposterous they are.

Enter LYSANDER and HELENA

LYSANDER

Why should you think that I should woo in scorn?

Why do you think I am mocking you when I woo you?

Scorn and derision never come in tears:

I wouldn't cry if I were making fun of you:

Look, when I vow, I weep; and vows so born,

Look how I cry as I pledge my love – pledges like this

In their nativity all truth appears.

Are born from honesty, and are thus true.

How can these things in me seem scorn to you,

160

How can you think that I am mocking you

Bearing the badge of faith, to prove them true?

When these things wear the badge of faith, my tears, to prove that they are real?

HELENA

You do advance your cunning more and more.

You are becoming more and more cunning.

When truth kills truth, O devilish-holy fray!

What a horrible thing it is when true vows run against opposite true vows!

These vows are Hermia's: will you give her o'er?

Your promises to Hermia – will you break them?

Weigh oath with oath, and you will nothing weigh:

Two oaths on opposing scales will balance out and lead you to neither decision:

Your vows to her and me, put in two scales,

Your promises to her, and now to me,

Will even weigh, and both as light as tales.

Weigh evenly – and I think they are as empty as myths.

LYSANDER

I had no judgment when to her I swore.

I was judging poorly when I swore my love to her.

HELENA

Nor none, in my mind, now you give her o'er.

And you have no judgment now, as you try to give her up.

LYSANDER

Demetrius loves her, and he loves not you.

Demetrius loves Hermia, anyway, he does not love you.

DEMETRIUS

[Awaking] O Helena, goddess, nymph, perfect, divine!

Oh Helena, goddess, fairy, perfect, divine!

To what, my love, shall I compare thine eyne?

What can I compare your beauty to?

Crystal is muddy. O, how ripe in show

Crystal is muddy. Oh your lips

Thy lips, those kissing cherries, tempting grow!

so ripe, like two cherries touching each other, are so tempting!

That pure congealed white, high Taurus snow,

The pure whiteness of a mountaintop's snow

Fann'd with the eastern wind, turns to a crow

Blown by the eastern wind turns as black as a crow

When thou hold'st up thy hand: O, let me kiss

When compared with your hand. Let me kiss

This princess of pure white, this seal of bliss!

You, a princess of pure white, and seal my happiness!

HELENA

O spite! O hell! I see you all are bent

Oh curses on both of you! You are both together

To set against me for your merriment:

Joined in mocking me for your own enjoyment.

If you were civil and knew courtesy,

If you were kind, and new common courtesy,

You would not do me thus much injury.

You wouldn't hurt me this much.

Can you not hate me, as I know you do,

Can you just hate me, as I know you do,

But you must join in souls to mock me too?

Without joining together to make fun of me as well?

If you were men, as men you are in show,

If you were true men, as noble as you pretend to be

You would not use a gentle lady so;

You would not treat a gentle lady like this:

To vow, and swear, and superpraise my parts,

To promise and swear your love, to overemphasize my beauty,

When I am sure you hate me with your hearts.

When I know that really you hate me in your hearts.

You both are rivals, and love Hermia;

You are rivals in loving Hermia,

And now both rivals, to mock Helena:

And now you are rivals in mocking me:

A trim exploit, a manly enterprise,

A neat and manly goal,

To conjure tears up in a poor maid's eyes

To create tears to fall from a poor girl's eyes

With your derision! none of noble sort

From your evilness! No truly noble man

Would so offend a virgin, and extort

Would cause such hurt in a young, chaste girl, none would test

A poor soul's patience, all to make you sport.

A poor soul's patience for his own fun.

LYSANDER

You are unkind, Demetrius; be not so;

You are mean, Demetrius, now stop.

For you love Hermia; this you know I know:

You love Hermia and you know that I know it,

And here, with all good will, with all my heart,

And right here, with the best of my intentions,

In Hermia's love I yield you up my part;

I give up my pursuit of Hermia.

And yours of Helena to me bequeath,

Now you give up your vows to Helena

Whom I do love and will do till my death.

Whom I love and will do so until I die.

HELENA

Never did mockers waste more idle breath.

Jokers never wasted so much breath in speaking nonsense.

DEMETRIUS

Lysander, keep thy Hermia; I will none:

Lysander, keep your Hermia because I will not.

If e'er I loved her, all that love is gone.

If I ever truly lover her, that love is now gone.

My heart to her but as guest-wise sojourn'd,

My heart journeyed to her, but did not stay,

And now to Helen is it home return'd,

And now it has come back to its home, Helena,

There to remain.

Where it will remain.

LYSANDER

Helen, it is not so.

Helena, he is lying.

DEMETRIUS

Disparage not the faith thou dost not know,

Don't insult the love you do not know

Lest, to thy peril, thou aby it dear.

Or else, to your harm, you will have to pay for your words.

Look, where thy love comes; yonder is thy dear.

Look, your love is coming from over there; there is your beloved.

Re-enter HERMIA

HERMIA

Dark night, that from the eye his function takes,

The night is so dark that it ruins the eye's ability to see,

The ear more quick of apprehension makes;

But it makes the ear's hearing stronger.

Wherein it doth impair the seeing sense,

Though it hurts one's sense of sight,

It pays the hearing double recompense.

It accounts for such harm by giving hearing twice as much perception.

Thou art not by mine eye, Lysander, found;

I could not find you, Lysander, by my sight,

Mine ear, I thank it, brought me to thy sound

But I thank my ears that brought me to your voice –

But why unkindly didst thou leave me so?

Why did you so abruptly leave my side?

LYSANDER

Why should he stay, whom love doth press to go?

Why should I have stayed, when love pressed me to go?

HERMIA

What love could press Lysander from my side?

What love could possibly press you to go and outweigh your love for me?

LYSANDER

Lysander's love, that would not let him bide,

My unabiding love for

Fair Helena, who more engilds the night

Beautiful Helena, who makes the night look more golden

Than all you fiery oes and eyes of light.

Than do the stars above.

Why seek'st thou me? could not this make thee know,

Why did you look for me? Didn't my leaving make it obvious

The hate I bear thee made me leave thee so?

That I hate you, and that this hate made me leave?

HERMIA

You speak not as you think: it cannot be.

You cannot be speaking what you really think.

HELENA

Lo, she is one of this confederacy!

Hermia is part of this plan to mock me!

Now I perceive they have conjoin'd all three

Now I see that all three have joined together

To fashion this false sport, in spite of me.

To play this mean joke at my expense.

Injurious Hermia! most ungrateful maid!

Hurtful Hermia! You awful lady!

Have you conspired, have you with these contrived

Have you planned with these men

To bait me with this foul derision?

To trick me with this mean ploy?

Is all the counsel that we two have shared,

Remember all that we shared, the conversations

The sisters' vows, the hours that we have spent,

And the promises, the hours spent together,

When we have chid the hasty-footed time

We were even angry that we didn't have more

For parting us,--O, is it all forgot?

Time together – and now is it all lost?

All school-days' friendship, childhood innocence?

Our friendship at school and our young innocent friendship, lost?

We, Hermia, like two artificial gods,

Hermia, we used to be like fake gods of our world,

Have with our needles created both one flower,

Sitting together and sewing the same flower

Both on one sampler, sitting on one cushion,

On the same sampler, sitting on the same cushion

Both warbling of one song, both in one key,

and singing together in the same key,

As if our hands, our sides, voices and minds,

As if our hands and bodies, our voices and our minds

Had been incorporate. So we grow together,

Were fused together. We grew together

Like to a double cherry, seeming parted,

Like two cherries – seemingly apart,

But yet an union in partition;

But united at the base,

Two lovely berries moulded on one stem;

Two lovely cherries joined at the stem.

So, with two seeming bodies, but one heart;

Seemingly we had two different bodies, but always one heart,

Two of the first, like coats in heraldry,

Like two coats of arms on a shield

Due but to one and crowned with one crest.

That pledge their allegiance to the same king, crowned with a single crest.

And will you rent our ancient love asunder,

And now will you break the bonds of all of this

To join with men in scorning your poor friend?

By joining with these men in mocking me?

It is not friendly, 'tis not maidenly:

It is neither friendly nor ladylike:

Our sex, as well as I, may chide you for it,

All women would do well to criticize you for it,

Though I alone do feel the injury.

Though I am the only woman hurt by it.

HERMIA

I am amazed at your passionate words.

What you are saying stuns me.

I scorn you not: it seems that you scorn me.

I do not hold you in contempt, but it seems you think of me that way.

HELENA

Have you not set Lysander, as in scorn,

Didn't you make Lysander, from your contempt for me,

To follow me and praise my eyes and face?

Follow me and compliment my looks?

And made your other love, Demetrius,

And then didn't you make the other man who loves you, Demetrius,

Who even but now did spurn me with his foot,

Who at all times before now turned me away, even with his foot,

To call me goddess, nymph, divine and rare,

Call me a goddess, a fairy, divine and rare,

Precious, celestial? Wherefore speaks he this

Precious and heavenly? Why else would he say this

To her he hates? and wherefore doth Lysander

To the one he hates? And why does Lysander

Deny your love, so rich within his soul,

Deny his love for you, which before was all he could talk about,

And tender me, forsooth, affection,

And now give me, really, signs of affection –

But by your setting on, by your consent?

Why else but from you consenting to it and asking him to do it?

What thought I be not so in grace as you,

What did you think, seeing me in such an unhappy position,

So hung upon with love, so fortunate,

So obsessed with love, so happy to be in love

But miserable most, to love unloved?

But all the more miserable to be in love without being loved in return?

This you should pity rather than despise.

You should pity me instead of mock me.

HERNIA

I understand not what you mean by this.

I don't know what you mean by what you are saying.

HELENA

Ay, do, persever, counterfeit sad looks,

Fine, continue your fake sadness,

Make mouths upon me when I turn my back;

And laugh silently at me when I turn around,

Wink each at other; hold the sweet jest up:

Wink at each other, keep up your joke.

This sport, well carried, shall be chronicled.

This game, carried out long enough, will be remembered.

If you have any pity, grace, or manners,

If you have any pity, grace, or manners,

You would not make me such an argument.

You would not make me even have to appeal like this.

But fare ye well: 'tis partly my own fault;

But have fun – it's all partly my own fault I guess,

Which death or absence soon shall remedy.

And death or running away will fix it soon enough.

LYSANDER

Stay, gentle Helena; hear my excuse:

Wait, Helena, hear what I have to say,

My love, my life my soul, fair Helena!

Dear love, the life of my soul, beautiful Helena!

HELENA

O excellent!

Great, more joking.

HERMIA

Sweet, do not scorn her so.

Darling, do not mock her like that.

DEMETRIUS

If she cannot entreat, I can compel.

If Hermia can't get you to stop, I can force you to.

LYSANDER

Thou canst compel no more than she entreat:

Your forcing will have no more strength than Hermia's pleas.

Thy threats have no more strength than her weak prayers.

Your threats are not stronger than her prayers.

Helen, I love thee; by my life, I do:

Helena, I swear by my life that I love you,

I swear by that which I will lose for thee,

And will lose that life for you,

To prove him false that says I love thee not.

Just to prove Demetrius wrong who says I do not love you.

DEMETRIUS

I say I love thee more than he can do.

I say I love you more than Lysander does.

LYSANDER

If thou say so, withdraw, and prove it too.

If you think so, then draw your sword and prove it.

DEMETRIUS

Quick, come!

172

Alright, come!

HERMIA

Lysander, whereto tends all this?

Lysander, why are you doing all of this?

LYSANDER

Away, you Ethiope!

Get away from me, African woman!

DEMETRIUS

No, no; he'll

No, he'll

Seem to break loose; take on as you would follow,

Pretend to leave you, Hermia. And you Lysander will pretend to fight

But yet come not: you are a tame man, go!

But will not advance toward me. You are a cowardly man, go away!

LYSANDER

Hang off, thou cat, thou burr! vile thing, let loose,

Get off of me, you cat, you thorn! Awful thing, let go of me,

Or I will shake thee from me like a serpent!

Hermia, or I will shake you off as if you are a serpent!

HERMIA

Why are you grown so rude? what change is this?

Why have you become so mean? What changed?

Sweet love,--

My love--

LYSANDER

Thy love! out, tawny Tartar, out!

Your love! No, get away, you black skinned Tartar!

Out, loathed medicine! hated potion, hence!

Out, evil medicine, hated potion!

HERMIA

Do you not jest?

Are you not joking?

HELENA

Yes, sooth; and so do you.

Yes, of course he is, and you are as well.

LYSANDER

Demetrius, I will keep my word with thee.

Demetrius, I will duel you now.

DEMETRIUS

I would I had your bond, for I perceive

I wish I believed your bond, for I see

A weak bond holds you: I'll not trust your word.

That you seem to make promises you break easily, so I won't trust your word.

LYSANDER

What, should I hurt her, strike her, kill her dead?

What must I do, hurt Hermia? Hit her? Kill her?

Although I hate her, I'll not harm her so.

Though I hate her, I will not do that.

HERMIA

What, can you do me greater harm than hate?

What harm can you do to me that is greater than hate?

Hate me! wherefore? O me! what news, my love!

Hate me! Why? Oh my! What has happened, my love?

Am not I Hermia? are not you Lysander?

Aren't I Hermia? Aren't you Lysander?

I am as fair now as I was erewhile.

I am just as beautiful as I was before.

Since night you loved me; yet since night you left me:

Since the night started you still loved me, but then you left me:

Why, then you left me--O, the gods forbid!--

Then you left me-- Oh God forbid!--

In earnest, shall I say?

Did you really? Must I admit that?

LYSANDER

Ay, by my life;

Yes, I did,

And never did desire to see thee more.

And I do not wish to see you again.

Therefore be out of hope, of question, of doubt;

Stop questioning and stop wondering, stop hoping:

Be certain, nothing truer; 'tis no jest

Be certain, because nothing is more true than this: I am not joking

That I do hate thee and love Helena.

That I hate you and love Helena.

HERMIA

O me! you juggler! you canker-blossom!

Oh my! Helena, you awful thorn!

You thief of love! what, have you come by night

You thief! Did you come in the night

And stolen my love's heart from him?

And steal Lysander's heart from me?

HELENA

Fine, i'faith!

That's a nice touch.

Have you no modesty, no maiden shame,

Have you no shame at all,

No touch of bashfulness? What, will you tear

No slight remorse? Are you trying to make me angry

Impatient answers from my gentle tongue?

In order to get me to say impatient and evil things?

Fie, fie! you counterfeit, you puppet, you!

Damn you! You fake, you puppet!

HERMIA

Puppet? why so? ay, that way goes the game.

Puppet? Why that? Oh now I see.

Now I perceive that she hath made compare

Helena has compared

Between our statures; she hath urged her height;

Our heights, and, taller, has praised her own height:

And with her personage, her tall personage,

Because she is tall, taller than me,

Her height, forsooth, she hath prevail'd with him.

She has convinced Lysander to love her instead.

And are you grown so high in his esteem;

Did you grow in his eyes because of this?

Because I am so dwarfish and so low?

Because I am so short, like a dwarf, and thus a person of lower quality?

How low am I, thou painted maypole? speak;

Well how low of a person am I, you who is as tall as a maypole?

How low am I? I am not yet so low

I know this much: I am not so short

But that my nails can reach unto thine eyes.

That I cannot scratch your eyes out with my nails.

HELENA

I pray you, though you mock me, gentlemen,

Please, men, though you are making fun of me,

Let her not hurt me: I was never curst;

Don't let her hurt me. I was never cursed at

I have no gift at all in shrewishness;

And am not good at being an evil woman.

I am a right maid for my cowardice:

It is better that I am a coward,

Let her not strike me. You perhaps may think,

But let her not hit me. You may think that

Because she is something lower than myself,

Because she is shorter

That I can match her.

I can fight her off.

HERMIA

Lower! hark, again.

See! She says "shorter" again.

HELENA

Good Hermia, do not be so bitter with me.

Hermia, do not be bitter with me.

I evermore did love you, Hermia,

I have always loved you, Hermia,

Did ever keep your counsels, never wrong'd you;

Always kept your secrets, never wronged you,

Save that, in love unto Demetrius,

Until this: because of my love for Demetrius

I told him of your stealth unto this wood.

I told him of your plans to run away into the forest.

He follow'd you; for love I follow'd him;

He followed you and for love I followed him,

But he hath chid me hence and threaten'd me

But then he turned me away and threatened

To strike me, spurn me, nay, to kill me too:

To hit me, no, even to kill me.

And now, so you will let me quiet go,

Now, let me quietly go away,

To Athens will I bear my folly back

Back to Athens where I will bring my mistakes with me

And follow you no further: let me go:

And will not follow you anymore. Let me go,

You see how simple and how fond I am.

You see see how simple and foolishly in love I am.

HERMIA

Why, get you gone: who is't that hinders you?

Then go: what keeps you here?

HELENA

A foolish heart, that I leave here behind.

A foolish heart that I must force myself to give up.

HERMIA

What, with Lysander?

Your love for Lysander?

HELENA

With Demetrius.

For Demetrius.

LYSANDER

Be not afraid; she shall not harm thee, Helena.

Do not fear, Helena, Hermia will not hurt you.

DEMETRIUS

No, sir, she shall not, though you take her part.

No, she won't, even if you, Lysander, try to help her.

HELENA

O, when she's angry, she is keen and shrewd!

Oh, she is so smart and vicious when she is angry!

She was a vixen when she went to school;

She was a vixen at school,

And though she be but little, she is fierce.

And though she is little, she can be fierce.

HERMIA

'Little' again! nothing but 'low' and 'little'!

"Little" again! You keep saying "low" and "little"!

Why will you suffer her to flout me thus?

Why do you both allow her to mock me like this?

Let me come to her.

Let me get to her.

LYSANDER

Get you gone, you dwarf;

Go away, you dwarf,

You minimus, of hindering knot-grass made;

You miniature thing made of grass,

You bead, you acorn.

You bead, you acorn.

DEMETRIUS

You are too officious

That is going to far,

In her behalf that scorns your services.

Especially for one who does not want your love or aid.

Let her alone: speak not of Helena;

Let Helena alone, do not speak for her

Take not her part; for, if thou dost intend

And stop taking Helena's side. If you continue

Never so little show of love to her,

To treat Hermia so poorly,

Thou shalt aby it.

You'll pay for it.

LYSANDER

Now she holds me not;

Hermia is nothing to me now.

Now follow, if thou darest, to try whose right,

Now, if you dare, follow me and let us see whose right,

Of thine or mine, is most in Helena.

Yours or mine, is Helena's love.

DEMETRIUS

Follow! nay, I'll go with thee, cheek by jole.

I will not follow – I will walk side by side with you.

Exeunt LYSANDER and DEMETRIUS

HERMIA

You, mistress, all this coil is 'long of you:

All of this fighting is because of you, Helena,

Nay, go not back.

Do not go back to Athens.

HELENA

I will not trust you, I,

I don't trust you, and I

Nor longer stay in your curst company.

Will no longer stay here in your awful company.

Your hands than mine are quicker for a fray,

You are more desirous of a fight,

My legs are longer though, to run away.

But my long legs are better for running away.

Exit

HERMIA

I am amazed, and know not what to say.

I am amazed, and don't know what to say.

Exit

OBERON

This is thy negligence: still thou mistakest,

This is your fault: either you made a mistake

Or else committ'st thy knaveries wilfully.

Or you are playing a prank on purpose.

PUCK

Believe me, king of shadows, I mistook.

Believe me, my king, I made a mistake.

Did not you tell me I should know the man

Remember that you told me I would recognize the man

By the Athenian garment be had on?

By his Athenian clothing?

And so far blameless proves my enterprise,

So far, I have done nothing wrong,

That I have 'nointed an Athenian's eyes;

Since I put the potion on an Athenian man's eyes.

And so far am I glad it so did sort

Though I am glad it all turned out like this,

As this their jangling I esteem a sport.

Since I find their fighting a fun game to watch.

OBERON

Thou see'st these lovers seek a place to fight:

You saw as well as I did that the men are looking for a place to fight,

Hie therefore, Robin, overcast the night;

So go, Puck, and make the night cloudy.

The starry welkin cover thou anon

Cover the starry sky

With drooping fog as black as Acheron,

With a low fog as dark as the Acheron River,

And lead these testy rivals so astray

And make these fighting men lose each other

As one come not within another's way.

So they do not end up dueling.

Like to Lysander sometime frame thy tongue,

Sometimes speak like Lysander

Then stir Demetrius up with bitter wrong;

And get Demetrius angry at being wronged,

And sometime rail thou like Demetrius;

And sometimes speak like Demetrius.

And from each other look thou lead them thus,

Like this keep them away from each other

Till o'er their brows death-counterfeiting sleep

Until they fall asleep, appearing almost like they are dead.

With leaden legs and batty wings doth creep:

Then, creep quietly up to them with bat's wings

Then crush this herb into Lysander's eye;

And put this antidote into Lysander's eye

Whose liquor hath this virtuous property,

Which will, by it's good qualities,

To take from thence all error with his might,

Remove the former potion

And make his eyeballs roll with wonted sight.

And make his eyes return to their natural sight.

When they next wake, all this derision

When they wake back up, all of this fighting

Shall seem a dream and fruitless vision,

Shall seem like a dream with no aftereffects,

And back to Athens shall the lovers wend,

And the lovers shall go back to Athens

With league whose date till death shall never end.

With their beloveds in order to marry them.

Whiles I in this affair do thee employ,

While you do this job,

I'll to my queen and beg her Indian boy;

I will go to Queen Titania and ask for her Indian boy

And then I will her charmed eye release

And then will give her eye the antidote so that she stops

From monster's view, and all things shall be peace.

Loving the monster, and finally all things will be peaceful.

PUCK

My fairy lord, this must be done with haste,

My king, this should be done quickly

For night's swift dragons cut the clouds full fast,

Since night is already fading quickly

And yonder shines Aurora's harbinger;

And far in the east the morning appears to be breaking.

At whose approach, ghosts, wandering here and there,

When that happens, the ghosts that wander about

Troop home to churchyards: damned spirits all,

Return to their homes in the graveyards, these damned spirits

That in crossways and floods have burial,

Who were not buried in holy grounds

Already to their wormy beds are gone;

Have already returned to their wormy graves.

For fear lest day should look their shames upon,

They are afraid that day will look at their shame

They willfully themselves exile from light

So they choose to stay away from the light

And must for aye consort with black-brow'd night.

And instead only come out at night.

OBERON

But we are spirits of another sort:

We are different spirits than them.

I with the morning's love have oft made sport,

I have often played in the morning with the morning's blessing

And, like a forester, the groves may tread,

And am allowed, like a hunter, to walk through the forests

Even till the eastern gate, all fiery-red,

186

Even until the east is as red as fire

Opening on Neptune with fair blessed beams,

And the sun rises over the oceans, its blessed beams

Turns into yellow gold his salt green streams.

Turning the salty green seawater golden yellow.

But, notwithstanding, haste; make no delay:

In any case, hurry along

We may effect this business yet ere day.

So that we can finish this work before day starts.

Exit

PUCK

Up and down, up and down,

Up and down, and back and forth,

I will lead them up and down:

I will lead them all over.

I am fear'd in field and town:

Those who live in the town and the fields are afraid of me.

Goblin, lead them up and down.

I am Goblin who will lead them all over.

Here comes one.

Here is one now.

Re-enter LYSANDER

LYSANDER

Where art thou, proud Demetrius? speak thou now.

Where are you, Demetrius? Tell me.

PUCK

Here, villain; drawn and ready. Where art thou?

Here, you villain, with my sword ready. Where are you?

LYSANDER

I will be with thee straight.

I will be near you soon enough.

PUCK

Follow me, then,

Follow me, then,

To plainer ground.

To a good ground for battle.

Exit LYSANDER, as following the voice

Re-enter DEMETRIUS

DEMETRIUS

Lysander! speak again:

Lysander, speak!

Thou runaway, thou coward, art thou fled?

You coward, have you run away?

Speak! In some bush? Where dost thou hide thy head?

Speak! Are you hiding in a bush? Where?

PUCK

Thou coward, art thou bragging to the stars,

You coward, are you bragging to the heavens

Telling the bushes that thou look'st for wars,

And telling all of the bushes that you are ready to fight,

And wilt not come? Come, recreant; come, thou child;

But will not come at me? Come, miscreant, come you child.

I'll whip thee with a rod: he is defiled

I will beat you with a stick. Whoever

That draws a sword on thee.

Pulls a sword on me will become insulted.

DEMETRIUS

Yea, art thou there?

Hey, where are you?

PUCK

Follow my voice: we'll try no manhood here.

Follow my voice, we will not fight here.

Exeunt

Re-enter LYSANDER

LYSANDER

He goes before me and still dares me on:

When I come where he calls, then he is gone.

The villain is much lighter-heel'd than I:

I follow'd fast, but faster he did fly;

That fallen am I in dark uneven way,

And here will rest me.

Lies down

Come, thou gentle day!

For if but once thou show me thy grey light,

I'll find Demetrius and revenge this spite.

Sleeps

Re-enter PUCK and DEMETRIUS

PUCK

Ho, ho, ho! Coward, why comest thou not?

Ha ha! Coward, why haven't you come yet?

DEMETRIUS

Abide me, if thou darest; for well I wot

Stay where you are, if you dare. I see

Thou runn'st before me, shifting every place,

You running ahead of me, changing your place,

And darest not stand, nor look me in the face.

Because you do not dare stop and stand up to me.

Where art thou now?

Now where are you?

190

PUCK

Come hither: I am here.

Come over here, I am here.

DEMETRIUS

Nay, then, thou mock'st me. Thou shalt buy this dear,

No, you are mocking me. You will pay for this

If ever I thy face by daylight see:

If I ever see you in the daylight.

Now, go thy way. Faintness constraineth me

Go along, I am too tired and must

To measure out my length on this cold bed.

Stretch out on the ground to sleep.

By day's approach look to be visited.

Prepare yourself to fight in the morning.

Lies down and sleeps

Re-enter HELENA

HELENA

O weary night, O long and tedious night,

Oh night that has been so long and tedious,

Abate thy hour! Shine comforts from the east,

Please end! Let the daylight break from the east

That I may back to Athens by daylight,

So that I can get back to Athens easily

From these that my poor company detest:

And leave these supposed friends who really hate me.

And sleep, that sometimes shuts up sorrow's eye,

Now I will sleep, and hope that sleep can quell my sorrow

Steal me awhile from mine own company.

By removing me from myself for a little.

Lies down and sleeps

PUCK

Yet but three? Come one more;

I've seen only three so far, where is the other?

Two of both kinds make up four.

Two men and two women make four for the company.

Here she comes, curst and sad:

Here comes Hermia, cursed and sad:

Cupid is a knavish lad,

Cupid is a mean prankster

Thus to make poor females mad.

To women feel this poorly.

Re-enter HERMIA

HERMIA

Never so weary, never so in woe,

I have never been this exhausted or this sad,

Bedabbled with the dew and torn with briers,

And I am wet with dew, and scratched by the thorns.

I can no further crawl, no further go;

I cannot crawl any farther, much less walk.

My legs can keep no pace with my desires.

My legs are not as strong as my desire to get back to Athens,

Here will I rest me till the break of day.

So I will rest here for the rest of the night, until morning.

Heavens shield Lysander, if they mean a fray!

God protect Lysander if there is a duel!

Lies down and sleeps

PUCK

On the ground

Sleep here

Sleep sound:

On the ground

I'll apply

While I put this potion

To your eye,

In your eye,

Gentle lover, remedy.

Gentle lover, and it will fix you.

Squeezing the juice on LYSANDER's eyes

When thou wakest,

When you wake,

Thou takest

You will feel

True delight

Your true love again

In the sight

After you see

Of thy former lady's eye:

Hermia, whom you formerly loved.

And the country proverb known,

The saying in the country

That every man should take his own,

That "Every man should take his own,"

In your waking shall be shown:

And you will prove this when you wake:

Jack shall have Jill;

Jack will love Jill

Nought shall go ill;

And neither shall be upset,

The man shall have his mare again, and all shall be well.

The man will have his lady again, and everything will be good.

Exit

Act IV

Scene I
The same. LYSANDER, DEMETRIUS, HELENA, and HERMIA lying asleep.

Enter TITANIA and BOTTOM; PEASEBLOSSOM, COBWEB, MOTH, MUSTARDSEED, and other Fairies attending; OBERON behind unseen

TITANIA

Come, sit thee down upon this flowery bed,

Come over here and sit on this bed of flowers

While I thy amiable cheeks do coy,

While I brush your smooth cheeks

And stick musk-roses in thy sleek smooth head,

And places flowers in your hair

And kiss thy fair large ears, my gentle joy.

And kiss your beautiful, large ears, my joy.

BOTTOM

Where's Peaseblossom?

Where's Peaseblossom?

PEASEBLOSSOM

Ready.

Here.

BOTTOM

Scratch my head Peaseblossom. Where's Mounsieur Cobweb?

Please scratch my head, Peaseblossom. And where is Monsieur Cobweb?

COBWEB

Ready.

Here.

BOTTOM

Mounsieur Cobweb, good mounsieur, get you your

Monsieur Cobweb, good monsieur, fetch

weapons in your hand, and kill me a red-hipped

your weapons and kill a red-striped

humble-bee on the top of a thistle; and, good

bumblebee sitting on the top of a thistle for me, and then,

mounsieur, bring me the honey-bag. Do not fret

monsieur, bring me honey from it. Do not worry

yourself too much in the action, mounsieur; and,

too much while you are doing this, monsieur, and,

good mounsieur, have a care the honey-bag break not;

good monsieur, try not to break the honey bag:

I would be loath to have you overflown with a

I would hate to see you covered with

honey-bag, signior. Where's Mounsieur Mustardseed?

honey, signior. Where's Monsieur Mustardseed?

MUSTARDSEED

Ready.

Here.

BOTTOM

Give me your neaf, Mounsieur Mustardseed. Pray you,

Give me your hand, Monsieur Mustardseed. Please,

leave your courtesy, good mounsieur.

do what I ask, good monsieur.

MUSTARDSEED

What's your Will?

What would you like me to do?

BOTTOM

Nothing, good mounsieur, but to help Cavalery Cobweb

Nothing, good monsieur, except to help Calvary Cobweb

to scratch. I must to the barber's, monsieur; for

scratch my head. I must go to a barber, monsieur, because

methinks I am marvellous hairy about the face; and I

I think my beard has grown out all around my face,

am such a tender ass, if my hair do but tickle me,

and my face is so tender that if hair only tickles it slightly,

I must scratch.

I must scratch it.

TITANIA

What, wilt thou hear some music,

Would you like to hear some music,

my sweet love?

my love?

BOTTOM

I have a reasonable good ear in music. Let's have

I have a good ear for music. Someone play

the tongs and the bones.

The triangle and the keys.

TITANIA

Or say, sweet love, what thou desirest to eat.

Or maybe, my love, you can say what you would like to eat.

BOTTOM

Truly, a peck of provender: I could munch your good

Really, a good bit of grass: I could munch on some

dry oats. Methinks I have a great desire to a bottle

dry oats. I think I really want a portion

of hay: good hay, sweet hay, hath no fellow.

of hay. There is nothing like good, sweet hay.

TITANIA

I have a venturous fairy that shall seek

I have a fairy that will find

The squirrel's hoard, and fetch thee new nuts.

The nuts a squirrel has hidden for winter, and will fetch you some of them.

BOTTOM

198

I had rather have a handful or two of dried peas.

I'd rather eat a handful or two of dried peas.

But, I pray you, let none of your people stir me: I

But, please, don't let your fairies wait on me now: I

have an exposition of sleep come upon me.

am feeling incredibly tired all of a sudden.

TITANIA

Sleep thou, and I will wind thee in my arms.

Then sleep, and I will put my arms around you.

Fairies, begone, and be all ways away.

Fairies, go away in all directions.

Exeunt fairies

So doth the woodbine the sweet honeysuckle

The woodbine plant and the honeysuckle

Gently entwist; the female ivy so

Wrap around each other just as I am doing to you. So does the female ivy

Enrings the barky fingers of the elm.

Wrapping around the bark trunk of the elm.

O, how I love thee! how I dote on thee!

I love you so much and want to give you so much!

They sleep

Enter PUCK

OBERON

[Advancing] Welcome, good Robin.

Hello, good Robin.

See'st thou this sweet sight?

Do you see this sweet picture?

Her dotage now I do begin to pity:

I'm starting to pity her affection

For, meeting her of late behind the wood,

Because, when I met her recently here in the forest,

Seeking sweet favours from this hateful fool,

She was looking for gifts for this fool,

I did upbraid her and fall out with her;

And I argued and fought with her.

For she his hairy temples then had rounded

She has placed around his hairy head

With a coronet of fresh and fragrant flowers;

A crown of fresh, good smelling flowers:

And that same dew, which sometime on the buds

And the dew that rests on the flower buds,

Was wont to swell like round and orient pearls,

Which sometimes looks like perfectly round pearls from the Far East,

Stood now within the pretty flowerets' eyes

Stood in the flowers

Like tears that did their own disgrace bewail.

Like tears, crying at the disgrace of being around the fool's head.

When I had at my pleasure taunted her

When I was done having my fun in taunting her

And she in mild terms begg'd my patience,

And she had begged me to stop,

I then did ask of her her changeling child;

I asked her of her orphan child

Which straight she gave me, and her fairy sent

Whom she immediately gave to me, and sent her fairy

To bear him to my bower in fairy land.

To take him to my room in fairy land.

And now I have the boy, I will undo

Now that I have the boy I will give her the antidote

This hateful imperfection of her eyes:

To remove this ugly infatuation.

And, gentle Puck, take this transformed scalp

Also, Puck, remove this donkey-head

From off the head of this Athenian swain;

From the head of the Athenian commoner

That, he awaking when the other do,

So that he, waking up when the others do,

May all to Athens back again repair

Can return to Athens again

And think no more of this night's accidents

And think nothing of the night's adventures,

But as the fierce vexation of a dream.

Regarding them only as a dream.

But first I will release the fairy queen.

First, I will cure Queen Titania.

Be as thou wast wont to be;

Be as you were

See as thou wast wont to see:

And see how you used to see:

Dian's bud o'er Cupid's flower

This flower of Diana's, the goddess of Virginity, against the flower struck by Cupid's arrow,

Hath such force and blessed power.

Has the blessed power to turn you to normal.

Now, my Titania; wake you, my sweet queen.

Now, Titania, wake up, my queen.

TITANIA

My Oberon! what visions have I seen!

Oberon! What dreams I have had!

Methought I was enamour'd of an ass.

I thought I was in love with a donkey.

OBERON

There lies your love.

Right there is who you loved.

TITANIA

How came these things to pass?

How did these things happen?

O, how mine eyes do loathe his visage now!

Oh, I can't stand the sight of him now.

OBERON

Silence awhile. Robin, take off this head.

Be quiet for a moment. Robin, remove the false head.

Titania, music call; and strike more dead

Titania, call for music, the kind that will make these people

Than common sleep of all these five the sense.

Sleep more soundly than the dead.

TITANIA

Music, ho! music, such as charmeth sleep!

Play music, fairies! The kind that creates sleep!

Music, still

PUCK

Now, when thou wakest, with thine

Now when you wake, you

own fool's eyes peep.

will look out with your human, but still foolish, eyes.

OBERON

Sound, music! Come, my queen, take hands with me,

Play, music! Come with me, my queen, hold my hand

And rock the ground whereon these sleepers be.

And dance with me to keep the sleepers alseep.

Now thou and I are new in amity,

We are friendly again

And will to-morrow midnight solemnly

And tomorrow at midnight

Dance in Duke Theseus' house triumphantly,

We will dance in Duke Theseus' house in celebration,

And bless it to all fair prosperity:

Blessing it for success.

There shall the pairs of faithful lovers be

And there, these pairs of faithful lovers

Wedded, with Theseus, all in jollity.

Will be married as well, along with Theseus, in happiness.

PUCK

Fairy king, attend, and mark:

King Oberon, listen –

I do hear the morning lark.

I do hear the morning bird.

OBERON

Then, my queen, in silence sad,

In that case, my queen, let us silently

Trip we after the night's shade:

Leave to wherever it is still night.

We the globe can compass soon,

We can go around the world

Swifter than the wandering moon.

Quicker than the moon does.

TITANIA

Come, my lord, and in our flight*Come, my king, and while we travel*

Tell me how it came this night

Tell me what happened this night,

204

That I sleeping here was found

How I was sleeping here

With these mortals on the ground.

With these humans on the ground next to me.

Exeunt

Horns winded within

Enter THESEUS, HIPPOLYTA, EGEUS, and train

THESEUS

Go, one of you, find out the forester;

One of you, go and find the forest manager.

For now our observation is perform'd;

Since we have finished our May Day rites

And since we have the vaward of the day,

And now have the beginning of the day in front of us,

My love shall hear the music of my hounds.

My love will hear the sound of hunting horns for my dogs.

Uncouple in the western valley; let them go:

Untie them in the valley and let them go.

Dispatch, I say, and find the forester.

I said leave and find the forest manager.

Exit an Attendant

We will, fair queen, up to the mountain's top,

We will go, beautiful queen, up to the mountain peak

And mark the musical confusion

And listen to the confusing sounds

Of hounds and echo in conjunction.

Of dogs barking and their barks echoing back.

HIPPOLYTA

I was with Hercules and Cadmus once,

I was with Hercules and Cadmus once

When in a wood of Crete they bay'd the bear

In a forest in Crete and their Spartan dogs

With hounds of Sparta: never did I hear

Surrounded a bear: I never heard

Such gallant chiding: for, besides the groves,

Such impressive barking. Besides the forest,

The skies, the fountains, every region near

The skies and fountains, and everywhere around us

Seem'd all one mutual cry: I never heard

Seemed to echo the barking in unison. I never heard

So musical a discord, such sweet thunder.

Such beautiful noise, such sweet thunder.

THESEUS

My hounds are bred out of the Spartan kind,

My hounds are bred from Spartan ones,

So flew'd, so sanded, and their heads are hung

With the same hanging lips and sandy colored coat, and their heads similarly hang

With ears that sweep away the morning dew;

With their ears low along the morning dew.

Crook-knee'd, and dew-lapp'd like Thessalian bulls;

206

They similarly have crooked knees, and neck folds like bulls from Thessaly.

Slow in pursuit, but match'd in mouth like bells,

They are slower in the chase, but they have the same bark, like bells

Each under each. A cry more tuneable

In their mouths. There was never a better sounding cry

Was never holla'd to, nor cheer'd with horn,

Cheered on with a hunting horn heard

In Crete, in Sparta, nor in Thessaly:

In Crete, Sparte, or Thessaly:

Judge when you hear. But, soft! what nymphs are these?

You can judge so when you hear them. But wait, who are these people?

EGEUS

My lord, this is my daughter here asleep;

My lord, this is my daughter Hermia, fast asleep,

And this, Lysander; this Demetrius is;

And this is Lysander, and this is Demetrius,

This Helena, old Nedar's Helena:

And this is Helena, Nedar's daughter.

I wonder of their being here together.

I wonder why they are all here together.

THESEUS

No doubt they rose up early to observe

They must have woken early in order to keep

The rite of May, and hearing our intent,

The rites of May Day, and, knowing my plans to celebrate it as well,

Came here in grace our solemnity.

Came here to join us.

But speak, Egeus; is not this the day

But Egeus: isn't today the day

That Hermia should give answer of her choice?

When Hermia must tell us how she answers?

EGEUS

It is, my lord.

Yes, it is, my lord.

THESEUS

Go, bid the huntsmen wake them with their horns.

Go, and tell the huntsmen to blow their horns to wake them.

Horns and shout within. LYSANDER, DEMETRIUS, HELENA, and HERMIA wake and start up

Good morrow, friends. Saint Valentine is past:

Good morning, friends. Valentine's day is past:

Begin these wood-birds but to couple now?

Shouldn't you lovebirds have paired up back then?

LYSANDER

Pardon, my lord.

Forgive us, my lord.

THESEUS

I pray you all, stand up.

Please, all of you stand up.

I know you two are rival enemies:

I know you two, Lysander and Demetrius, are rivals,

How comes this gentle concord in the world,

So how is there this peace in the world

That hatred is so far from jealousy,

And how in your jealousy did you not hate each other,

To sleep by hate, and fear no enmity?

To the point where you could sleep next to each other and not be afraid of wrongdoing?

LYSANDER

My lord, I shall reply amazedly,

My lord, I am rather confused, but I will reply

Half sleep, half waking: but as yet, I swear,

In my half-sleep, half-woken state. So far, I promise,

I cannot truly say how I came here;

I don't really know how I came here.

But, as I think,--for truly would I speak,

But I think, -- well I want to tell you the truth

And now do I bethink me, so it is,--

And now that I think about it, I think this is true --

I came with Hermia hither: our intent

I came here with Hermia, in order to

Was to be gone from Athens, where we might,

Run away from Athens, to wherever we could,

Without the peril of the Athenian law.

So that we would not have to face the dangers of the Athenian law.

EGEUS

Enough, enough, my lord; you have enough:

My lord, you've heard enough already:

I beg the law, the law, upon his head.

Now I beg you to enforce the law and punish him.

They would have stolen away; they would, Demetrius,

They would have run away, they would have, Demetrius,

Thereby to have defeated you and me,

And thus would have defeated both of us,

You of your wife and me of my consent,

Stealing your wife, and my consent,

Of my consent that she should be your wife.

My consent that Hermia should be your wife.

DEMETRIUS

My lord, fair Helen told me of their stealth,

My lord, Helena told me of their plans

Of this their purpose hither to this wood;

And their purpose for coming to the forest,

And I in fury hither follow'd them,

And I furiously followed them,

Fair Helena in fancy following me.

Beautiful Helena, out of love for me, following me.

But, my good lord, I wot not by what power,--

But, my lord, I do not know what power changed me --

But by some power it is,--my love to Hermia,

Though it is certainly a strong power -- but this power changed my love for Hermia,

Melted as the snow, seems to me now

And melted it away, like snow, so that now

As the remembrance of an idle gaud

I remember it as a worthless trinket

Which in my childhood I did dote upon;

That I loved when I was still a child.

And all the faith, the virtue of my heart,

And now, all of my heart and soul finds

The object and the pleasure of mine eye,

As its sole pleasure

Is only Helena. To her, my lord,

Only Helena. I was, my lord,

Was I betroth'd ere I saw Hermia:

Meant to marry her before I ever saw Hermia,

But, like in sickness, did I loathe this food;

But as if I were sick and rejecting good food, I rejected this too.

But, as in health, come to my natural taste,

Now I am healthy and returned to my natural tastes,

Now I do wish it, love it, long for it,

And I wish for, love, and long for Helena,

And will for evermore be true to it.

And will forevermore be faithful to her.

THESEUS

Fair lovers, you are fortunately met:

Fair lovers, it is fortunate we met here.

Of this discourse we more will hear anon.

We will hear more about this soon.

Egeus, I will overbear your will;

Egeus, I must override your request:

For in the temple by and by with us

In the temple with Hippolyta and me

These couples shall eternally be knit:

These two couples will be wed for eternity.

And, for the morning now is something worn,

And as the morning is almost passed,

Our purposed hunting shall be set aside.

We will put our hunting trip on hold for another time.

Away with us to Athens; three and three,

Let us go to Athens now: three men and three women to marry,

We'll hold a feast in great solemnity.

Well we will have a great feast together.

Come, Hippolyta.

Let us go, Hippolyta.

Exeunt THESEUS, HIPPOLYTA, EGEUS, and train

DEMETRIUS

These things seem small and undistinguishable,

Everything from last night looks small, and hard to make out,

Like far-off mountains turnèd into clouds.

Like a mountain far away that looks like distant clouds.

HERMIA

Methinks I see these things with parted eye,

I feel like I see the everything as blurry,

When every thing seems double.

Or in double vision.

HELENA

So methinks:

Yes, me too.

And I have found Demetrius like a jewel,

I feel like Demetrius is a jewel I have found,

Mine own, and not mine own.

And is thus mine, but also not mine, that someone else could claim him at any time.

DEMETRIUS

Are you sure

Is it certain

That we are awake? It seems to me

That we are all awake? It feels like

That yet we sleep, we dream. Do not you think

We are still asleep and dreaming. Was the duke

The duke was here, and bid us follow him?

Really here, and did he ask us to follow him?

HERMIA

Yea; and my father.

Yes, my father was here as well.

HELENA

And Hippolyta.

And Hippolyta.

LYSANDER

And he did bid us follow to the temple.

And he asked us to go to the temple with him.

DEMETRIUS

Why, then, we are awake: let's follow him

Well we are definitely awake, then. Let's follow Duke Theseus

And by the way let us recount our dreams.

And tell each other our dreams as we walk.

Exeunt

BOTTOM

[Awaking] When my cue comes, call me, and I will

Tell me when it is my cue and I will

answer: my next is, 'Most fair Pyramus.' Heigh-ho!

say my line – the next one is "Most fair Pyramus." Hello!

Peter Quince! Flute, the bellows-mender! Snout,

Peter Quince! Flute, the bellows-repairman! Snout,

the tinker! Starveling! God's my life, stolen

The repairman! Starveling! My God, they have left

hence, and left me asleep! I have had a most rare

while I was asleep! I had the strangest

vision. I have had a dream, past the wit of man to

dream. It is outside of the abilities of mankind

say what dream it was: man is but an ass, if he go

to explain it: a man is as foolish as a donkey if he tries to

about to expound this dream. Methought I was--there

explain the dream of mine. I thought I was -- well

is no man can tell what. Methought I was,--and

no one can really say what exactly. I thought I was -- and I

methought I had,--but man is but a patched fool, if

thought I had -- but someone would be an idiot to

he will offer to say what methought I had. The eye

say what I thought I had. A man's eye

of man hath not heard, the ear of man hath not

has not heard, his ear has not

seen, man's hand is not able to taste, his tongue

seen, his hand cannot taste, and his tongue

to conceive, nor his heart to report, what my dream

cannot touch, nor his heart explain, what my dream

was. I will get Peter Quince to write a ballad of

was. I will ask Peter Quince to write a ballad song

this dream: it shall be called Bottom's Dream,

about my dream and will call it "Bottom's Dream,"

because it hath no bottom; and I will sing it in the

because it doesn't have a bottom, and I will sing it

latter end of a play, before the duke:

at the end of the play, in front of the duke.

peradventure, to make it the more gracious, I shall

In fact, to make it even more lovely, I will

sing it at her death.

sing it when Thisby dies.

Exit

Scene II
Athens. QUINCE'S house.

Enter QUINCE, FLUTE, SNOUT, and STARVELING

QUINCE

Have you sent to Bottom's house ? is he come home yet?

Have you been to Bottom's house? Is he home yet?

STARVELING

He cannot be heard of. Out of doubt he is

No one has heard anything. I'm certain he has been

transported.

taken.

FLUTE

If he come not, then the play is marred: it goes

If he does not come, then the play is ruined – it

not forward, doth it?

can't go forward, right?

QUINCE

It is not possible: you have not a man in all

It's impossible – no one in all

Athens able to discharge Pyramus but he.

of Athens can play Pyramus convincingly except for Bottom.

FLUTE

No, he hath simply the best wit of any handicraft

I agree – he is the smartest of all handymen

man in Athens.

in Athens.

QUINCE

Yea and the best person too; and he is a very

Yes, and the best looking man, as well. And he is a very

paramour for a sweet voice.

paramour for a sweet voice.

FLUTE

You must say 'paragon:' a paramour is, God bless us,

You mean "paragon," a paramour is

a thing of naught.

something bad.

Enter SNUG

SNUG

Masters, the duke is coming from the temple, and

Everyone, the duke is leaving the temple, and

there is two or three lords and ladies more married:

two or three more men and women were married.

if our sport had gone forward, we had all been made

If we could have performed our play, we would have been rich

218

men.

men.

FLUTE

O sweet bully Bottom! Thus hath he lost sixpence a

Oh that Bottom! He has not lost getting paid sixpence

day during his life; he could not have 'scaped

every day of his life, I'm sure he would have been forced to take

sixpence a day: an the duke had not given him

sixpence a day, and if the duke would not have given him

sixpence a day for playing Pyramus, I'll be hanged;

sixpence a day for his performance of Pyramus, I would have hung myself.

he would have deserved it: sixpence a day in

Bottom would have deserved sixpence a day

Pyramus, or nothing.

to play Pyramus, or it's nothing.

Enter BOTTOM

BOTTOM

Where are these lads? where are these hearts?

Where are you boys, where are you friends?

QUINCE

Bottom! O most courageous day! O most happy hour!

Bottom! Oh great timing, what a wonderful day!

BOTTOM

Masters, I am to discourse wonders: but ask me not

Friends, I have many odd things to tell you, but do not

what; for if I tell you, I am no true Athenian. I

ask me what they are. If I tell you, I am not an Athenian, and so I won't.

will tell you every thing, right as it fell out.

Or I will tell you everything, just as it happened.

QUINCE

Let us hear, sweet Bottom.

Please tell us, Bottom.

BOTTOM

Not a word of me. All that I will tell you is, that

I will not tell you a single word except that

the duke hath dined. Get your apparel together,

the duke has eaten. Get your costumes together,

good strings to your beards, new ribbons to your

tie the beards on with good strings, and put new ribbons

pumps; meet presently at the palace; every man look

on your shows. We must go immediately to the palace. Everyone

o'er his part; for the short and the long is, our

look over your lines because, basically, the duke

play is preferred. In any case, let Thisby have

wants to hear our play. Anyway, give Thisby the

clean linen; and let not him that plays the lion

clean clothes and do not clip the nails of him who plays

pair his nails, for they shall hang out for the

the lion, for they should look like

lion's claws. And, most dear actors, eat no onions

lion claws. Oh, and actors: do not eat onions

nor garlic, for we are to utter sweet breath; and I

or garlic, because our breath should smell good. I

do not doubt but to hear them say, it is a sweet

am sure they will all say that ours is a pleasant and sweet

comedy. No more words: away! go, away!

comedy. I have nothing else to say, now go, get ready!

Exeunt

Act V

Scene I
Athens. The palace of THESEUS.

Enter THESEUS, HIPPOLYTA, PHILOSTRATE, Lords and Attendants

HIPPOLYTA

'Tis strange my Theseus, that these

It's a strange story, Theseus, that these

lovers speak of.

lovers tell.

THESEUS

More strange than true: I never may believe

More strange than it is true, I think. I will never believe

These antique fables, nor these fairy toys.

These old tales or fairy stories.

Lovers and madmen have such seething brains,

Both lovers and madmen are able to

Such shaping fantasies, that apprehend

Hallucinate and see such things, things

More than cool reason ever comprehends.

That cool, collected reason would never see.

The lunatic, the lover and the poet

The crazy person, lover, and poet

Are of imagination all compact:

Share heightened imaginations:

222

One sees more devils than vast hell can hold,

One sees demons everywhere, more than are even in hell,

That is, the madman: the lover, all as frantic,

And that is the crazy person. The lover, just as crazy,

Sees Helen's beauty in a brow of Egypt:

Sees unimaginable beauty, like that of ancient Helen, in an Egyptian's face.

The poet's eye, in fine frenzy rolling,

And the poet, in a frenzy,

Doth glance from heaven to earth, from earth to heaven;

Looks from heaven to earth, and from earth to heaven,

And as imagination bodies forth

And just as imagination creates in one's mind

The forms of things unknown, the poet's pen

The form of things that do not exist, the poet by writing

Turns them to shapes and gives to airy nothing

Describes their shapes and gives a name

A local habitation and a name.

And a place things that are really nothing.

Such tricks hath strong imagination,

These people have such strong imaginations

That if it would but apprehend some joy,

That if they think of some joy they want,

It comprehends some bringer of that joy;

They then believe that that joy has arrived.

Or in the night, imagining some fear,

Or, at nighttime, they might imagine something scary

How easy is a bush supposed a bear!

And believe that the bush is a bear!

HIPPOLYTA

But all the story of the night told over,

But the story these lovers are telling of the night,

And all their minds transfigured so together,

And how they all say the same things,

More witnesseth than fancy's images

Seems to point to more than just imagined images

And grows to something of great constancy;

And becomes something very consistent –

But, howsoever, strange and admirable.

But whatever the truth, it is a story both strange and interesting.

THESEUS

Here come the lovers, full of joy and mirth.

Here come the lovers, happy and joyful.

Enter LYSANDER, DEMETRIUS, HERMIA, and HELENA

Joy, gentle friends! joy and fresh days of love

Joy to you, my friends! I wish joy and days full of love

Accompany your hearts!

for your hearts!

LYSANDER

More than to us

224

We wish you more joy, which

Wait in your royal walks, your board, your bed!

Will be with you in your royal walks, your dinner table, and your bed!

THESEUS

Come now; what masques, what dances shall we have,

Now what dances and performances will we have

To wear away this long age of three hours

In order to fill the three hours

Between our after-supper and bed-time?

Between our dinner and our bedtime?

Where is our usual manager of mirth?

Where is the one who manages the entertainment?

What revels are in hand? Is there no play,

What fun is in store for us? Isn't there a play

To ease the anguish of a torturing hour?

To fill this torturous boredom?

Call Philostrate.

Call Philostrate to me.

PHILOSTRATE

Here, mighty Theseus.

I am here, mighty Theseus.

THESEUS

Say, what abridgement have you for this evening?

Tell me, what entertainment did you plan for the evening?

What masque? what music? How shall we beguile

What play or music? How will we pass

The lazy time, if not with some delight?

This lazy time if now with something fun?

PHILOSTRATE

There is a brief how many sports are ripe:

Here is a list of what entertainment is available:

Make choice of which your highness will see first.

Choice whichever your highness would like first.

Giving a paper

THESEUS

[Reads] 'The battle with the Centaurs, to be sung

"The battle between Hercules and the Centaurs, sung

By an Athenian eunuch to the harp.'

By an Athenian eunuch while playing the harp."

We'll none of that: that have I told my love,

Not that one: I told that story to Hippolyta

In glory of my kinsman Hercules.

To praise my friend Hercules.

Reads

'The riot of the tipsy Bacchanals,

"The riots of the drunken Bacchanals

Tearing the Thracian singer in their rage.'

226

Who rip apart the singer from Thrace, Orpheus, in their rage."

That is an old device; and it was play'd

This is an old tale: I saw it

When I from Thebes came last a conqueror.

When I came from Thebes as a conqueror.

Reads

'The thrice three Muses mourning for the death

"Nine Muses mourning for the death

Of Learning, late deceased in beggary.'

Of Learning and Knowledge, deceased after being poor."

That is some satire, keen and critical,

This seems to be a satire, very analytical,

Not sorting with a nuptial ceremony.

And not matching the mood of a wedding ceremony.

Reads

'A tedious brief scene of young Pyramus

A tedious brief scene of young Pyramus

And his love Thisbe; very tragical mirth.'

And his love Thisbe; very sad happiness."

Merry and tragical! tedious and brief!

Happy and sad! Tedious, but still brief!

That is, hot ice and wondrous strange snow.

That's like hot ice, and strange snow.

How shall we find the concord of this discord?

What is the harmony to this disharmony? How do these things fit together?

PHILOSTRATE

A play there is, my lord, some ten words long,

Yes, that is a play, my lord, of about ten words long,

Which is as brief as I have known a play;

As brief as any play I have ever known.

But by ten words, my lord, it is too long,

But these ten words are ten too many,

Which makes it tedious; for in all the play

Which makes the play tedious. In the whole play,

There is not one word apt, one player fitted:

Not a single word is the right one, nor one actor adept.

And tragical, my noble lord, it is;

Tragic and sad, my lord, it certainly is,

For Pyramus therein doth kill himself.

For Pyramus kills himself in the play.

Which, when I saw rehearsed, I must confess,

This event, when I saw it rehearsed, I must be honest,

Made mine eyes water; but more merry tears

Made me cry – but happier tears

The passion of loud laughter never shed.

Has my loud laughter never cried like these.

THESEUS

What are they that do play it?

Who are the actors?

PHILOSTRATE

Hard-handed men that work in Athens here,

Common workers and handymen in Athens,

Which never labour'd in their minds till now,

Who never tried working their minds until now,

And now have toil'd their unbreathed memories

And now have overworked their minds

With this same play, against your nuptial.

With this play for your wedding.

THESEUS

And we will hear it.

Then we will hear it.

PHILOSTRATE

No, my noble lord;

No, my noble lord,

It is not for you: I have heard it over,

This is not the play for you. I have heard it

And it is nothing, nothing in the world;

And it is worth nothing, nothing at all,

Unless you can find sport in their intents,

Unless you would enjoy watching their attempts to perform,

Extremely stretch'd and conn'd with cruel pain,

Their bad acting and the memorization that must have cost them much pain,

To do you service.

And then it might suit you.

THESEUS

I will hear that play;

That is the play I want,

For never anything can be amiss,

Since nothing can be wrong

When simpleness and duty tender it.

When simple people try and work hard in something.

Go, bring them in: and take your places, ladies.

Bring them in front of us. Ladies, take your seats.

Exit PHILOSTRATE

HIPPOLYTA

I love not to see wretchedness o'er charged

I do not like to see poor people asked to go above their capabilities

And duty in his service perishing.

And fail in their attempts to do something right.

THESEUS

Why, gentle sweet, you shall see no such thing.

Why, my dear, you will not see such a thing.

HIPPOLYTA

He says they can do nothing in this kind.

230

Philostrate says they cannot act or perform well at all.

THESEUS

The kinder we, to give them thanks for nothing.

Then we are kind to thank them for giving us nothing.

Our sport shall be to take what they mistake:

It will be fun to accept their mistakes,

And what poor duty cannot do, noble respect

And anyway, noble people should judge what duty and hard work cannot accomplish

Takes it in might, not merit.

By its attempts, not by its artistic merit.

Where I have come, great clerks have purposed

I have traveled to places where brilliant thinkers have tried

To greet me with premeditated welcomes;

To greet me with planned out and memorized speeches,

Where I have seen them shiver and look pale,

And time after time I watched them get nervous and become pale,

Make periods in the midst of sentences,

Stutter and stop in the middle of their sentences,

Throttle their practised accent in their fears

Mess up their formal tones from being afraid,

And in conclusion dumbly have broke off,

And finally end their speeches prematurely,

Not paying me a welcome. Trust me, sweet,

In the end not even welcoming me. Trust me,

Out of this silence yet I pick'd a welcome;

From their silence and awkwardness I still saw their intent to welcome me,

And in the modesty of fearful duty

And in their humbleness that made them afraid,

I read as much as from the rattling tongue

I saw just as much of a welcoming speech as I do from those who speak easily

Of saucy and audacious eloquence.

And give creative, loud, eloquent speeches.

Love, therefore, and tongue-tied simplicity

Thus, someone who loves but still falters in their simple speech

In least speak most, to my capacity.

Means most to me and can say the most, even when saying the least.

Re-enter PHILOSTRATE

PHILOSTRATE

So please your grace, the Prologue is address'd.

If you are ready, my grace, the prologue is ready to be given.

THESEUS

Let him approach.

Let him start.

Flourish of trumpets

Enter QUINCE for the Prologue

Prologue

If we offend, it is with our good will.

If we offend you, know that we offend you out of our desire to.

That you should think, we come not to offend,

Or, in other words, we haven't come to offend you,

But with good will. To show our simple skill,

But we came to bother you most with our good intentions. To show the talent of our performance

That is the true beginning of our end.

This is the beginning of our deaths.

Consider then we come but in despite.

Recognize that we are coming here in spite of.

We do not come as minding to contest you,

We do not come here to make you oppose you,

Our true intent is. All for your delight

Our true goal. For your happiness,

We are not here. That you should here repent you,

We didn't come. That you should be forced to apologize,

The actors are at hand and by their show

The actors are ready to make you do that, and from the play

You shall know all that you are like to know.

You will find out everything you are meant to know.

THESEUS

This fellow doth not stand upon points.

This man doesn't see the actual punctuation.

LYSANDER

He hath rid his prologue like a rough colt; he knows

He read the prologue like one riding an unbroken horse, not knowing not the stop. A good moral, my lord: it is not

when to stop. A good lesson, my lord: just

enough to speak, but to speak true.

speaking is not good enough – it is also important to speak well, with good grammar.

HIPPOLYTA

Indeed he hath played on his prologue like a child

Yes, he spoke that prologue like a child

on a recorder; a sound, but not in government.

playin a recorder – all sounds with no coherence.

THESEUS

His speech, was like a tangled chain; nothing

His speech was like a knotted and tangled chain: nothing

impaired, but all disordered. Who is next?

was wrong with the actual speech, but the parts were all jumbled. Who is next?

Enter Pyramus and Thisbe, Wall, Moonshine, and Lion

Prologue (QUINCE)

Gentles, perchance you wonder at this show;

Gentlemen and ladies, you might be confused at this play,

But wonder on, till truth make all things plain.

But continue to think on it and everything will be clear.

This man is Pyramus, if you would know;

This man is Pyramus,

This beauteous lady Thisby is certain.

And this beautiful lady is Thisby.

This man, with lime and rough-cast, doth present

234

This man covered with cement and gravel is

Wall, that vile Wall which did these lovers sunder;

the Wall, the evil Wall which separated the lovers

And through Wall's chink, poor souls, they are content

who, through a small hole in the Wall, they had to

To whisper. At the which let no man wonder.

whisper. So that should clear up his part.

This man, with lanthorn, dog, and bush of thorn,

And this man, with the lantern, dog, and thornbush,

Presenteth Moonshine; for, if you will know,

Is playing the Moonshine – since, you know,

By moonshine did these lovers think no scorn

It was by the moon that these lovers without shame

To meet at Ninus' tomb, there, there to woo.

met at Ninus' tomb, in order to court.

This grisly beast, which Lion hight by name,

This ugly animal, which we call a lion,

The trusty Thisby, coming first by night,

Saw Thisby, after she came to the tomb on the first night,

Did scare away, or rather did affright;

And scared her away, and frightened her severely.

And, as she fled, her mantle she did fall,

As she ran away, her cloak fell off

Which Lion vile with bloody mouth did stain.

And the evil Lion chewed on it with an already bloody mouth.

Anon comes Pyramus, sweet youth and tall,

Quickly after came Pyramus, a tall and handsome youth,

And finds his trusty Thisby's mantle slain:

Who saw Thisby's cloak bloodied,

Whereat, with blade, with bloody blameful blade,

And, with his bloody, angry sword,

He bravely broach'd is boiling bloody breast;

He bravely thrust it into his chest.

And Thisby, tarrying in mulberry shade,

Thisby, hiding in the shade of a mulberry tree

His dagger drew, and died. For all the rest,

Saw this and took Pyramus' dagger, and kill herself. For the rest of the story

Let Lion, Moonshine, Wall, and lovers twain

I will let Lion, Moonshine, Wall, and the two lovers

At large discourse, while here they do remain.

Speak about it, since they are right here.

Exeunt Prologue, Thisbe, Lion, and Moonshine

THESEUS

I wonder if the lion be to speak.

I wonder if the lion will speak.

DEMETRIUS

No wonder, my lord: one lion may, when many asses do.

Why not? Why shouldn't one lion speak when these donkeys have already.

Wall

In this same interlude it doth befall

At this time, it is worth repeating

236

That I, one Snout by name, present a wall;

That I am playing a wall (my real name is Snout).

And such a wall, as I would have you think,

The wall I am portraying, please believe,

That had in it a crannied hole or chink,

Has a hole in it

Through which the lovers, Pyramus and Thisby,

That the lovers Pyramus and Thisby

Did whisper often very secretly.

Whisper through secretly.

This loam, this rough-cast and this stone doth show

This stone and gravel all around me should make it clear

That I am that same wall; the truth is so:

That I am that wall, and truly,

And this the cranny is, right and sinister,

The hole is right here, each side of it,

Through which the fearful lovers are to whisper.

And through it the lovers will whisper.

THESEUS

Would you desire lime and hair to speak better?

Can cement ever speak better?

DEMETRIUS

It is the wittiest partition that ever I heard

It is the smartest room divider that I have ever heard

discourse, my lord.

converse, my lord.

Enter Pyramus

THESEUS

Pyramus draws near the wall: silence!

Pyramus is going near the wall, be quiet!

Pyramus

O grim-look'd night! O night with hue so black!

Oh night that looks so grim and black!

O night, which ever art when day is not!

Oh night, which is always there when the day is not!

O night, O night! alack, alack, alack,

Oh night, oh night! I am so sad, so sad,

I fear my Thisby's promise is forgot!

Because I am afraid Thisby forgot her promise!

And thou, O wall, O sweet, O lovely wall,

And you, oh sweet and wonderful wall,

That stand'st between her father's ground and mine!

You stand between her father's property and mine!

Thou wall, O wall, O sweet and lovely wall,

You, sweet and wonderful wall, dear wall,

Show me thy chink, to blink through with mine eyne!

Show me the hole that I can look through with my eye!

Wall holds up his fingers

Thanks, courteous wall: Jove shield thee well for this!

Thank you, kind wall. God protect you for this!

But what see I? No Thisby do I see.

But what do I see? Not Thisby.

O wicked wall, through whom I see no bliss!

Oh evil wall, I cannot see my happiness through you!

Cursed be thy stones for thus deceiving me!

Damn your stones for tricking me!

THESEUS

The wall, methinks, being sensible, should curse again.

Since it is a speaking wall, it should reply to Pyramus with a curse.

Pyramus

No, in truth, sir, he should not. 'Deceiving me'

Not really, my lord, he shouldn't because "Deceiving me"

is Thisby's cue: she is to enter now, and I am to

is the cue for Thisby to enter so that I can

spy her through the wall. You shall see, it will

see her through the wall. You'll see, everything

fall pat as I told you. Yonder she comes.

will happen like I said. Here she comes.

Enter Thisbe

THISBE

O wall, full often hast thou heard my moans,

Oh wall, you have heard my sad moans so often, blaming you

For parting my fair Pyramus and me!

For separating Pyramus and me!

My cherry lips have often kiss'd thy stones,

I have often kissed your stones with my lips as red as cherries,

Thy stones with lime and hair knit up in thee.

Your stones, stuck together with cement.

PYRAMUS

I see a voice: now will I to the chink,

I see something, now I will go to the hole

To spy an I can hear my Thisby's face. Thisby!

And see if I can hear Thisby's face. Thisby!

THRISBE

My love thou art, my love I think.

You are my love, I think.

PYRAMUS

Think what thou wilt, I am thy lover's grace;

Think whatever you want, I am your love:

And, like Limander, am I trusty still.

Just as faithful as heroic Limander.

THISBE

And I like Helen, till the Fates me kill.

And I will be as faithful as Helen of Troy, until the Fates decide my death.

PYRAMUS

Not Shafalus to Procrus was so true.

240

Not even Shafalus was as faithful to Procus.

THISBE

As Shafalus to Procrus, I to you.

Yes, I am like Shafalus to Procrus to you too.

PYRAMUS

O kiss me through the hole of this vile wall!

Oh kiss me through the hole of this evil wall!

THISBE

I kiss the wall's hole, not your lips at all.

I can only kiss the hole in the wall, I can't get to your lips.

Pyramus

Wilt thou at Ninny's tomb meet me straightway?

Then will you come meet me at Ninny's tomb right now?

THISBE

'Tide life, 'tide death, I come without delay.

I will come at once, and neither life nor death can stop me.

Exeunt Pyramus and Thisbe

WALL

Thus have I, Wall, my part discharged so;

Thus, I as Wall have finished my part,

And, being done, thus Wall away doth go.

And since I am done, Wall will leave as well.

Exit

THESEUS

Now is the mural down between the two neighbours.

And now the wall is down that separated the lovers.

DEMETRIUS

No remedy, my lord, when walls are so wilful to hear

There's nothing to do about it, lord, when walls will hear and speak

without warning.

without warning.

HIPPOLYTA

This is the silliest stuff that ever I heard.

This is the silliest play I've ever heard.

THESEUS

The best in this kind are but shadows; and the worst

The best plays are just illusions of reality, and so the worst

are no worse, if imagination amend them.

are not really worse – you just need imagination to fix them.

HIPPOLYTA

It must be your imagination then, and not theirs.

But it must be the audience's imagination, instead of the performers.

242

THESEUS

If we imagine no worse of them than they of

If we imagine them as they think

themselves, they may pass for excellent men. Here

of themselves, then they will look like the best of all men. Here

come two noble beasts in, a man and a lion.

come two very noble beasts: a man and a lion.

Enter Lion and Moonshine

LION

You, ladies, you, whose gentle hearts do fear

Dear ladies, whose gentle hears might be afraid

The smallest monstrous mouse that creeps on floor,

Of the smallest mouse creeping along the floor,

May now perchance both quake and tremble here,

You might now be tremble with fear,

When lion rough in wildest rage doth roar.

After an angry lion roars.

Then know that I, one Snug the joiner, am

Please know that I am really Snug the wood worker,

A lion-fell, nor else no lion's dam;

not really a fierce lion or a lioness.

For, if I should as lion come in strife

If I were a lion, and came angrily

Into this place, 'twere pity on my life.

To this place, I would be giving up my life.

THESEUS

A very gentle beast, of a good conscience.

What a kind beast, very caring for others.

DEMETRIUS

The very best at a beast, my lord, that e'er I saw.

The best actor I've ever seen portray a lion, my lord.

LYSANDER

This lion is a very fox for his valour.

This lion is as brave as a fox.

THESEUS

True; and a goose for his discretion.

And as wise as a goose.

DEMETRIUS

Not so, my lord; for his valour cannot carry his

No, my lord, because his courage doesn't make him

discretion; and the fox carries the goose.

wiser – as would be suggested since a fox carries a goose.

THESEUS

His discretion, I am sure, cannot carry his valour;

Well his wisdom certainly can't carry his courage,

244

for the goose carries not the fox. It is well:

which makes sense, since the goose can't carry the fox. Well,

leave it to his discretion, and let us listen to the moon.

we will leave the matter to his wisdom to resolve. I want to hear the moon.

MOONSHINE

This lanthorn doth the horned moon present;--

This lantern is the crescent moon above--

DEMETRIUS

He should have worn the horns on his head.

Then he should have worn horns on his head.

THESEUS

He is no crescent, and his horns are

This is no crescent moon, unless the horns

invisible within the circumference.

are invisible within the moon itself.

MOONSHINE

This lanthorn doth the horned moon present;

This lantern is the crescent moon above

Myself the man i' the moon do seem to be.

And I am the man in the moon.

THESEUS

This is the greatest error of all the rest: the man

They certainly made a mistake here: the actor

should be put into the lanthorn. How is it else the

should have been placed inside the lantern. How else would he be

man i' the moon?

the man in the moon?

DEMETRIUS

He dares not come there for the candle; for, you

He cannot go in there because of the candle;

see, it is already in snuff.

it is already charred and smoking.

HIPPOLYTA

I am aweary of this moon: would he would change!

I am tired of this moon and want it to change phases.

THESEUS

It appears, by his small light of discretion, that

It looks like, since he is not very bright,

he is in the wane; but yet, in courtesy, in all

he is waning, but we should be polite

reason, we must stay the time.

and see for certain.

LYSANDER

Proceed, Moon.

Continue, Moon.

MOONSHINE

All that I have to say, is, to tell you that the

All I have to say is that the

lanthorn is the moon; I, the man in the moon; this

lantern is the moon, I am the man in the moon,

thorn-bush, my thorn-bush; and this dog, my dog.

this bush of thorns is mine, and this dog is mine.

DEMETRIUS

Why, all these should be in the lanthorn; for all

Well all of these things should be inside the lantern then,

these are in the moon. But, silence! here comes Thisbe.

since they are in the moon. But wait! here comes Thisbe.

Enter Thisbe

THISBE

This is old Ninny's tomb. Where is my love?

This is old Ninny's tomb, but where is Pyramus, my love?

LION

[Roaring] Oh--

Roar!

Thisbe runs off

DEMETRIUS

Well roared, Lion.

Great roaring, Lion.

THESEUS

Well run, Thisbe.

Great running, Thisbe.

HIPPOLYTA

Well shone, Moon. Truly, the moon shines with a

Great shining, Moon. Really, the moon shines

good grace.

very beautifully.

The Lion shakes Thisbe's mantle

THESEUS

Well moused, Lion.

Well shaken, like a cat shaking a mouse, Lion.

DEMETRIUS

And then came Pyramus.

And now Pyramus enters.

Enter Pyramus

LYSANDER

And so the lion vanished.

248

And the lion is gone.

Exit Lion

PYRAMUS

Sweet Moon, I thank thee for thy sunny beams;

Dear Moon, thank you for your bright beams,

I thank thee, Moon, for shining now so bright;

Thank you for shining so brightly right now,

For, by thy gracious, golden, glittering gleams,

Because by your golden and shimmering beams

I trust to take of truest Thisby sight.

I can see Thisby even better.

But stay, O spite!

But wait, Oh no!

But mark, poor knight,

What is this, poor me,

What dreadful dole is here!

What is this awful thing!

Eyes, do you see?

Eyes, do you see what it is?

How can it be?

How is it possible?

O dainty duck! O dear!

Oh dainty duck! Oh dear!

Thy mantle good,

Your good cloak

What, stain'd with blood!

is what, it is stained with blood!

Approach, ye Furies fell!

Come you Furies, and avenge me!

O Fates, come, come,

Come you Fates, come,

Cut thread and thrum;

And cut the thread of my life,

Quail, crush, conclude, and quell!

Crush, finish, kill!

THESEUS

This passion, and the death of a dear friend, would

Such passion of an actor, next to the death of a close friend,

go near to make a man look sad.

could make someone very sad while watching this.

HIPPOLYTA

Beshrew my heart, but I pity the man.

I blame my heart, but I actually feel sorry for this man.

PYRAMUS

O wherefore, Nature, didst thou lions frame?

Oh Nature, why did you create lions?

Since lion vile hath here deflower'd my dear:

An evil lion has eaten my love

Which is--no, no--which was the fairest dame

250

Who is – no – who was the most beautiful woman

That lived, that loved, that liked, that look'd with cheer.

Who lived, loved, and was happy.

Come, tears, confound;

Come out tears, and overflow;

Out, sword, and wound

Come out sword, and hurt

The pap of Pyramus;

My chest –

Ay, that left pap,

Yes, the left part of the chest

Where heart doth hop:

Where my heart beats.

Stabs himself

Thus die I, thus, thus, thus.

This is how I will die, like this, like this.

Now am I dead,

Now I am dead

Now am I fled;

And running from this life.

My soul is in the sky:

My soul is already in heaven.

Tongue, lose thy light;

Tongue, it is time to stop talking.

Moon take thy flight:

Moon, leave me in the dark.

Exit Moonshine

Now die, die, die, die, die.

Now I die, die, die, die, die.

Dies

DEMETRIUS

No die, but an ace, for him; for he is but one.

We may not have dice around, but he is a die with a single dot, since he is only one person.

LYSANDER

Less than an ace, man; for he is dead; he is nothing.

Less than that even: since he is dead, he has no dots, he is nothing.

THESEUS

With the help of a surgeon he might yet recover, and

A doctor could perhaps help him and bring him back as

prove an ass.

a donkey.

HIPPOLYTA

How chance Moonshine is gone before Thisbe comes

Why is the Moon gone before Thisbe returns

back and finds her lover?

and finds Pyramus? How will she find him?

THESEUS

She will find him by starlight. Here she comes; and

By starlight, I suppose. Here she comes, and

her passion ends the play.

the play ends with her passion.

Re-enter Thisbe

HIPPOLYTA

Methinks she should not use a long one for such a

I dont think Thisbe should grieve too long for such a ridiculous

Pyramus: I hope she will be brief.

Pyramus, and I hope that she is quick.

DEMETRIUS

A mote will turn the balance, which Pyramus, which

So far it is even as to whether Pyramus

Thisbe, is the better; he for a man, God warrant us;

or Thisbe is better. God help us if he is a better man,

she for a woman, God bless us.

and God help us if she is a better woman.

LYSANDER

She hath spied him already with those sweet eyes.

She has already seen him with those pretty eyes.

DEMETRIUS

And thus she means, videlicet:--

And, as follows, she will——

THISBE

Asleep, my love?

My love, are you asleep?

What, dead, my dove?

Or are you dead?

O Pyramus, arise!

Pyramus get up!

Speak, speak. Quite dumb?

Please speak, can you not speak?

Dead, dead? A tomb

Are you really dead? In a tomb

Must cover thy sweet eyes.

You should be placed then, your beautiful eyes closed.

These My lips,

These lips of yours that were mine,

This cherry nose,

Your red nose

These yellow cowslip cheeks,

And your yellow cheeks like cowslip flowers,

Are gone, are gone:

Are gone!

Lovers, make moan:

Lovers, cry with me.

His eyes were green as leeks.

His eyes were green, like leeks.

O Sisters Three,

O Fates, the three Sisters,

Come, come to me,

Come to me

With hands as pale as milk;

With your pale hands

Lay them in gore,

And place them in the red gore of his body

Since you have shore

Since you have cut

With shears his thread of silk.

His life's thread with your scissors.

Tongue, not a word:

Tongue, be silent,

Come, trusty sword;

Come, sword of Pyramus,

Come, blade, my breast imbrue:

Come, blade, and enter my chest.

Stabs herself

And, farewell, friends;

Goodbye friends,

Thus Thisby ends:

Thus Thisby dies,

Adieu, adieu, adieu.

Goodbye, goodbye, goodbye.

Dies

THESEUS

Moonshine and Lion are left to bury the dead.

So Moonshine and Lion must bury the bodies.

DEMETRIUS

Ay, and Wall too.

Yes, and Wall.

BOTTOM

[Starting up] No assure you; the wall is down that

No, really: the wall that parted them

parted their fathers. Will it please you to see the

was taken down. Would you like to hear

epilogue, or to hear a Bergomask dance between two

the epilogue, or hear and watch a dance from two

of our company?

of our group?

THESEUS

No epilogue, I pray you; for your play needs no

Please, no epilogue, the play doesn't need

excuse. Never excuse; for when the players are all

an excuse. There's no point, anyway: since everyone

dead, there needs none to be blamed. Marry, if he

is dead, no one needs to be blamed. Actually, if you

that writ it had played Pyramus and hanged himself

had written that Pyramus had hanged himself

in Thisbe's garter, it would have been a fine

with Thisbe's belt, then it would have been a great

tragedy: and so it is, truly; and very notably

tragedy. Anyway, it was still very well

discharged. But come, your Bergomask: let your

done. Now, your dance – leave your

epilogue alone.

epilogue alone.

A dance

The iron tongue of midnight hath told twelve:

The bell is ringing out that it is midnight,

Lovers, to bed; 'tis almost fairy time.

So lovers, head to your beds. It's time for the fairies to come out.

I fear we shall out-sleep the coming morn

I am worried that we will sleep in and miss the morning

As much as we this night have overwatch'd.

Since we have been awake so late tonight.

This palpable-gross play hath well beguiled

This incredibly awful play has given a light air

The heavy gait of night. Sweet friends, to bed.

To the heaviness of the night. My friends, let us go to bed.

A fortnight hold we this solemnity,

We will continue this ceremony for two weeks,

In nightly revels and new jollity.

With nightly parties and new entertainments.

Exeunt

Scene II

259

Enter PUCK

PUCK

Now the hungry lion roars,

Now the hungry lion roars

And the wolf behowls the moon;

And the wolf howls at the moon,

Whilst the heavy ploughman snores,

While the fat farmer snores

All with weary task fordone.

Tired from his work.

Now the wasted brands do glow,

The used up firewood glows in the fireplace

Whilst the screech-owl, screeching loud,

While the owl, screeching loudly,

Puts the wretch that lies in woe

Reminds the man who is sick

In remembrance of a shroud.

Of the shroud of impending death.

Now it is the time of night

Now is the time of the night

That the graves all gaping wide,

When the graves open

Every one lets forth his sprite,

And out of every one comes a ghost

In the church-way paths to glide:

To glide along the paths of the graveyard.

And we fairies, that do run

And we fairies, who follow

By the triple Hecate's team,

Hecate the goddess of magic,

From the presence of the sun,

And must run from the sun

Following darkness like a dream,

To follow darkness like a dream,

Now are frolic: not a mouse

Want to frolic. But for now not a single mouse

Shall disturb this hallow'd house:

Will disturb this special house.

I am sent with broom before,

I was sent with a broom

To sweep the dust behind the door.

To clean up everything for the king and queen.

Enter OBERON and TITANIA with their train

OBERON

Through the house give gathering light,

The house has a little light still

By the dead and drowsy fire:

From the dying fire.

Every elf and fairy sprite

All the elves and fairies with us,

Hop as light as bird from brier;

Walk lightly, like a bird stepping around thorns,

And this ditty, after me,

And sing this song with me,

Sing, and dance it trippingly.

Sing and dance joyfully.

TITANIA

First, rehearse your song by rote

First, rehearse your song by remembering

To each word a warbling note:

Each word and the note that goes with it.

Hand in hand, with fairy grace,

Now, join hands, and with the grace of fairies

Will we sing, and bless this place.

We will sing while we bless this house.

Song and dance

OBERON

Now, until the break of day,

Now, until morning,

Through this house each fairy stray.

Go through all the corners of the house.

To the best bride-bed will we,

Titania and I will go to the bed of Hippolyta and Theseus

Which by us shall blessed be;

And bless it,

And the issue there create

And the children conceived there

Ever shall be fortunate.

Will always be fortunate and lucky.

So shall all the couples three

In fact, all three couples will be fortunate

Ever true in loving be;

And always faithful to each other.

And the blots of Nature's hand

The flaws that Nature sometimes produces

Shall not in their issue stand;

Will not exist in their children:

Never mole, hare lip, nor scar,

No moles, no cleft lips or scars,

Nor mark prodigious, such as are

No abnormal markings that are

Despised in nativity,

So ugly and hated at birth

Shall upon their children be.

Will ever appear on their children.

With this field-dew consecrate,

Take this dew from the fields,

Every fairy take his gait;

Each one of you,

And each several chamber bless,

And bless each room

Through this palace, with sweet peace;

Throughout the palace with peace.

And the owner of it blest

And the palace owner will be blessed

Ever shall in safety rest.

With safety.

Trip away; make no stay;

Go along and don't take too long,

Meet me all by break of day.

And meet me again at dawn.

Exeunt OBERON, TITANIA, and train

PUCK

If we shadows have offended,

If we fairies have offended you,

Think but this, and all is mended,

Then it will help you to think

That you have but slumber'd here

That you have fallen asleep here

While these visions did appear.

When you saw these visions.

And this weak and idle theme,

Consider this weak story

No more yielding but a dream,

Only a dream,

Gentles, do not reprehend:

Gentlemen and ladies, and do not be upset with me.

if you pardon, we will mend:

Forgive us and we will fix everything,

And, as I am an honest Puck,

And, since I am an honest Puck,

If we have unearned luck

If we have the good fortune

Now to 'scape the serpent's tongue,

Not to be hissed at,

We will make amends ere long;

We will make it up to you before long –

Else the Puck a liar call;

Or, you can call me a liar.

So, good night unto you all.

Goodnight to you all.

Give me your hands, if we be friends,

If you are friends, clap for me,

And Robin shall restore amends.

And I will make it all up to you.

About BookCaps

We all need refreshers every now and then. Whether you are a student trying to cram for that big final, or someone just trying to understand a book more, BookCaps can help. We are a small, but growing company, and are adding titles every month.

Visit www.bookcaps.com to see more of our books, or contact us with any questions.

Made in the USA
Middletown, DE
27 August 2021